Fostering Changes

Treating Attachment-Disordered Foster Children

Richard J. Delaney, Ph.D.

i

To Dick and Agnes
my parents and ever-available attachment figures.

To Margaret, Katie and Claire
my wife and daughters, who remained attached to me
through all of this.

And finally to the
caseworkers, foster parents and foster children
who have educated me about attachment-disorders.

Published by:

Wood 'N' Barnes Publishing
2717 NW 50th
Oklahoma City, OK 73112
(405)946-0621

Printed in the United States of America
Oklahoma City, Oklahoma
ISBN#1-885473-19-2

Cover sketches by Katie Gentry
Cover design by Blu Phillips

To order copies of Dr. Delaney's
books, please call:
Jean Barnes Books
800-678-0621

What people are saying about Fostering Changes...

"This book has spearheaded an understandable and meaningful way for treatment foster parents to improve their ability to work with troubled kids who need therapeutic treatment."
Doug Kuhn, PhD, LPC, Director, National Institute for Alternative Care Professionals (NIFACP)

"Dr. Delaney is passionate about his work! **Fostering Changes** communicates his hands-on experience and knowledge in dealing with attachment disorders in a way that is meaningful for all foster parents and professionals who work with children suffering from issues of attachment and bonding."
Druann Whitaker, MS, LSW, LPC, Chief Operating Officer, SAFY of America

"Dr. Delaney gives clear descriptions of the many children in foster care placement with attachment disorder. **Fostering Changes** addresses foster parents' full spectrum of feelings when dealing with attachment-disordered foster children. It is an excellent resource for training foster parents, giving a clear easily understood format for foster parents that want to learn more about the children in their care. The inclusion of the foster parent as part of the treatment team working with attachment-disordered foster children gives value to the whole system of care. I recommend **Fostering Changes** to anyone who cares for children in the child welfare system. The chances of working with children with attachment disorder is almost a given with the numbers of placement disruptions that occur with foster children."
Bonnie McNulty, Foster Parent for 33 years, Region VIII Vice-president of National Foster Parent Association, CEO of Presidio, Inc. a child placement agency.

"We have been foster parents to 27 children in the past 5 years, and adopted 3 of those precious children. Our home normally consists of our 5 energetic kids, plus 1 or more foster children. I also serve on the Permanency Planning Review Board for our county (seeing and hearing the cases of all the foster children in our county).
It would have been great to have had this book five years ago, when I started foster care. It is such a useful tool for sorting out the many odd behaviors, not normally experienced in societies' so called

normal homes. As I read through the book, I marked the many parts that I have experienced with several different children with a red pen - to say the least, there are lots of phrases underlined in red. Most important to me was (page 14/Concluding Remarks) *'Attachment between infant and caretaker is prerequisite to physical survival and emotional health of the child.'* And that I must continually remember (page 22) *'In essence, the negative internal working model is unfairly superimposed upon any subsequent intimate relationships, though its relationship to the reality of the new relationship may be non-existent.'* Thanks to Dr. Delaney for bringing this knowledge into our own homes, without having to spend countless hours with a therapist to try to get across what we are dealing with. It gives us a clearer picture of some of the children (not all) and helps put all the scattered pieces of several different behaviors together to make some sense of where they come from and why.

If DHS required reading for foster parents, **Fostering Changes** would have to be at the top of the list. I would highly recommend it to all new and current foster parents to read. Even if they don't have a child with AD right now they probably have in the past or will in the future. What a great tool to better understanding and giving a child a better chance in placement/life.

Dr. Delaney does an excellent job in giving real life examples of what he is talking about, with past case histories which give the reader a better understanding into the disorder he is talking about. I was enlightened and relieved to read that I am not alone in having dealt with children with attachment-disorder; and calmed to hear that other foster parents deal with some of the same emotions and responses toward AD children.

Fostering Changes has given me insight and useful knowledge to impart more understanding to what I am dealing with when trying to express to others (social workers, therapists, etc.) what is going on with a child that might possibly have attachment disorder.

The book hit so close to home it's scary. It has given me a better perspective from which to work and a point at which to start."

Terry L. Bullard, Foster and Adoptive Parent

Preface

Today's foster parents find themselves caring for — and trying to cope with — very emotionally disturbed foster children. Consensus among veteran caseworkers and foster parents is that there has been an upsurge in foster children with significant psychological problems. Previously, these children had been treated only in in-patient settings, e.g. on psychiatric wards or in residential child care facilities. Now, many of them are diverted into therapeutic or treatment foster homes, which are deemed to be the "least restrictive alternative," i.e. the most humane residence for young children. Disturbed foster children have often been the victims of child abuse, neglect, sexual exploitation and abandonment. Indeed, virtually every foster child has suffered some loss, disruption, and trauma prior to placement in foster care. Many have experienced severe,repeated, chronic maltreatment at the hands of their birth parents, relatives, or other caretakers.

By the time foster parents become involved with these unfortunate children, tremendous psychological damage has already been done. Though these children can be removed from the source of abuse and neglect, they take with them the invisible, internal scars of early maltreatment. Foster parents are not only left with the task of providing a safe home but also a therapeutic environment for these foster children. On the surface, that might appear to be a fairly straightforward job: to provide physically and psychologically for hapless, dependent, young human beings. However, many foster families soon find themselves faced with a task more challenging than they ever dreamed. In fact, the dream of helping an abused child can often turn into a nightmare. The foster parents, beleaguered by the child's severe, confusing, and sometimes alarming emotional and behavioral problems, find themselves asking, "Where did our plans for helping this child go?" or "How did we get ourselves into this mess, and how can we get out of it?"

Caseworkers, mental health professionals and others involved in helping the child can also become caught up in this bad dream. The mental health professional, often entering the picture too late, may find himself under pressure to quickly treat the child and foster family before the placement is totally ruined. He may wonder why the foster family describes the foster child so differently than he views him. He might wonder, "Is this foster family causing disturbance in this child or vice versa?" And the caseworker finds himself under the gun, and confronted by the foster parents who ask, "Why didn't you tell us how disturbed this child was?" or "Can you move this child to a new placement as soon as possible?"

Yes, the emotionally disturbed foster child brings many serious questions to mind. His conduct is often confused and confusing. His resistance to accepting help from the foster family, caseworker, and mental health professional is exasperating and, at times bewildering. In the saddest cases, these foster children sabotage placements in rapid succession. They thwart attempts to help them; they stymie all best efforts to reach them, to connect with them, and to heal those invisible scars. Sadly, in dealing with these taxing children, we are often left with more questions than answers.

Fortunately, many answers can be found in "attachment theory," a theory which stresses the importance of early caretaking for later psychological health. Since the early 1950's, attachment theory has proposed that disruption in reliable caretaking of young children results in defective or disordered attachment, i.e., the emotional bond linking caretaker and child (Bowlby, 1969). Defective attachments, in turn, beget psychological problems in the child which may span a lifetime. Unfortunately, though research abounds concerning attachment, few guidelines are offered to foster parents, caseworkers, and mental health professionals for their crucial work with children having significant attachment disorders. The source of the problem appears to be "extrapolation gap" i.e. failures in translating research data into specifics for individuals on the firing line: those attempting to help attachment-disordered foster children.

To address the gap, this book will translate information from controlled laboratory studies and from scarce clinical findings to the day-to-day work with attachment-disordered foster children. *Fostering Changes* provides a concise interpretation of the key principles of attachment theory. It then moves on to the issue of how attachment disorders form in maltreated children. It also addresses the sometimes bewildering array of conduct problems and other symptoms which children with attachment disorders show us while in foster placement. Ultimately, this book presents to the foster parent, caseworker, and mental health professional novel ways to intervene with the foster child, which can defeat his sabotaging behavior patterns.

Those who work with disturbed foster children are often the victims of the child's sabotage of placement, intimacy, and efforts to help him. Sabotage often appears in certain hallmark conduct problems — stealing, lying, sexual acting-out, fire-setting, passive-aggression, among others (see Appendix) — which can effectively undermine the stability of the foster placement and, in the process, interfere with the curative efforts aimed at the underlying attachment disorder.

As we will discuss ahead, conduct problems in foster children emerge from defects or anomalies in attachment formation, which render these children abnormally attached. Importantly, defective attachment formation produces in the child's mind distorted, cynical, overanxious perceptions (a negative "internal working model" or mental representation) of the world in general and caretakers in particular. After the child is placed, the foster parents fall heir to unfriendly perceptions which grew out of the child's past contact with abusive, neglectful, and/or exploitive parents (or caretakers).

Overview of the Book

To set the stage for later discussions on attachment-disordered foster children, Chapter One begins with a brief introduction to notions of attachment theory which are relevant to interventions with foster children. We discuss the survival function of attachment; the stages of normal attachment formation; and the characteristics of the securely attached child. The chapter ends with a discussion of the effect of disruption on the process of attachment and with a description of the types of abnormal attachments which develop in children following significant disruptions.

Chapter Two focuses on maltreated (i.e. abused, neglected, exploited) foster children and the notion of the "internal working model," the mental snapshot of oneself and his caretakers. We contrast here the internal working model of the securely attached child with that of the maltreated, abnormally attached child. Lastly, this chapter relates conduct problems in the attachment-disordered foster child to his underlying working model, i.e. to the child's skewed, stubbornly held, negative perceptions of caretakers and himself.

In Chapter Three we take further the discussion of the disturbed foster child's negative "working model" and how this "mental snapshot" of the world pushes the child into reenactment, i.e. recreating old relationships in the context of the foster home. The foster child's frequent and severe conduct problems— often confusing and bewildering taken individually—can more easily be understood when we see them as part of the overall reenactment process. (The Appendix provides very thorough descriptions of typical conduct problems which are seen in seriously disturbed, attachment-disordered foster children.)

Chapter Four outlines the common foster parent reactions to the foster child's attempts to reenact. Here we discuss the frighteningly abusive impulses which foster parents feel in these situations. We also discuss how foster mothers and fathers often can experience a foster child very differently. Special emphasis is placed on the central importance of the foster placement to outcomes with attachment-disordered foster children.

Chapter Five focuses on treatment of the attachment-disordered foster child. Specifically, we focus on the process of altering the negative working model which underlies conduct problems and reenactment. We discuss a four-part procedure, which includes the following: containing conduct problems; increasing verbalizations of the underlying negative working model; fostering negotiation skills; and promoting positive encounters between the foster parents and the child. Treatment, as outlined in this book, entails close collaboration between the foster parents and the psychotherapist.

Fostering Changes focuses on the treatment of elementary school-aged foster children who are in long-term placement, i.e. one year or more. Some of these foster children are free for adoption but deemed to be unadoptable, due to their conduct problems and underlying attachment disorders. Others of these foster children are not yet free for adoption, as the rights of their birth parents have not yet been terminated by the court system. The children we focus on this book do not, for the most part, have visits with their biological parents, and they are not destined to ever return to live with them. Of course, many foster children are placed short-term; ultimately do return to their parents; and have on-going visitations with them during placement. While attachment theory can, undoubtedly, be applied to treatment of these foster children, for simplicity sake, a discussion of that group has been omitted from this volume.

A word about the case examples in this book. In the interests of protecting confidentiality and concealing identities of the many foster children and families I have worked with over the years, I have scrupulously developed "psychological composites," which present the flavor of typical and bona fide cases without revealing actual names, places, histories, outcomes, and other details of the original children and families treated. Thus, any resemblance of these cases or the names used herein to actual children and families is due either to mere coincidence or to the sad fact that the traumatic histories and common symptoms of maltreated children form a familiar, recognizable mosaic.

Acknowledgements

Finally, I would like to express my deepest gratitude to a number of individuals who were vital to the completion of this book. They are Frank R. Kunstal, Ed.D; James Wm. Browning, M.D.; Mike DeWitt, Elisabeth Braun, Enita Kearns, Lee Phillips, and Margaret Delaney. I would like to thank them, my good friends and colleagues, who have tirelessly read and re-read the manuscript which became this book. While their frank reflections and suggestions have added immeasurably to the quality of the finished product, I am solely responsible for any remaining problems with the book's contents. In addition, I must pay my respects to the luminaries in research on attachment theory: John Bowlby, Mary Salter-Ainsworth, Jay Belsky, Mary Main, Matthew Speltz, Inge Bretherton, Alan Stroufe, and Mark Greenberg. However, while I have drawn heavily from their notions regarding attachment, the finished product of this book is in no way meant to summarize or reflect their thinking. The work of these researchers has provided a springboard to my own thinking, as has also the work of T. Berry Brazelton, Selma Fraiberg, Margaret Mahler, Erik Erikson, Melitta Sperling, Jerome Kagan, Vera Colburn-Fahlberg, Foster Cline, Ken Magid, Norman Polansky, and James Masterson.

Fort Collins, Colorado
Richard J. Delaney
April, 1991

Table of Contents

1 Brief Introduction to Attachment Theory

Before launching into a discussion of theory, consider this specific case:

* * * * *

Candy, a wisp of a Caucasian girl, had lived in nine different foster homes by her present age of six. Horribly malnourished as an infant, she was diagnosed as "failure to thrive" by a doctor at the health department. A neglected and delayed child, Candy was too weak to hold her head up at six months of age. She crawled at fourteen months and finally walked and talked (in garbled, one-word utterances) at two-years-old. Following frequent reports of neglect, unsanitary living conditions, and abandonment by the mother, Candy was placed in foster care on several occasions by the local welfare agency; and by her third birthday this child had spent seventy-five percent of her life in foster care. During her brief stays with the biological mother—between foster placements—Candy was often left for days in the care of the maternal grandmother, neighbors, and numerous babysitters, when the mother disappeared periodically with drug abusing men she was dating. When the birth mother, an apathetic, depressed woman for the most part, was present with Candy, it was usually between boyfriends. "Between boyfriends," this woman was even more depressed than usual and drank heavily, slept on the couch day and night, leaving Candy to fend for herself.

To compound the problem, when Candy was removed from the mother's care, she — due to an unfortunate set of circumstances — was placed in four different foster homes. In her fourth placement, Candy was described by the foster parents as "unlikeable," "unrewarding," and "unattached." They mentioned that she called them, "Daddy" and "Mommy" immediately after meeting them; but they felt that even after six months in their home, she would walk off with any stranger. Following this half-year placement, Candy was returned to her birth mother for one last try. Once again, Candy, nearly four years old, was left with a host of surrogate parent figures, when her mother disappeared for days and sometimes weeks. Reports of neglect prompted caseworkers to remove Candy once and for all. By this time, Candy, now in her fifth foster home, seemed much more disturbed and started showing a number of behavior problems. She lied, stole food, and urinated in the corner of her bedroom. The foster family described her as "fakey" and as "not a real child — a phoney." They portrayed her as sometimes withdrawn and rejecting of them and at other times very needy and draining.

Eventually, a psychologist was called in to do a thorough evaluation of this child and found Candy to suffer from a sense of powerlessness, underlying insecurities, and lack of empathy for others. She was also depicted as having "problems with attachment." Psychotherapy was recommended and started for Candy, but it was too late to save the foster placement, and the two others that followed in quick succession. Candy seemed to be "blowing out" placements as quickly as she arrived in the homes. By now she (age five) was living in her eighth foster home, which had to move from the area. On her sixth birthday, Candy was placed in her ninth foster home — a therapeutic foster home with parents specially trained to work with "attachment-disordered" children.

* * * * *

The purpose of this chapter is to set the stage for later discussions on the treatment of attachment-disordered foster children like Candy. To understand attachment-disorders, one first needs a grounding in what normal attachment is, what its purpose is, how it develops in human beings, and how it can go wrong. With that in mind, this chapter will provide a quick historical overview of attachment theory, a definition of attachment, and some examples of normal attachment behaviors in children and their caretakers. Following this, the four stages of attachment formation are presented along with the characteristics of the child who has successfully passed through these stages. Focus then shifts to the factors which disrupt the normal attachment process. The chapter ends with a description of the types of abnormal attachment young children develop in response to chronic disruptions in the attachment process.

Historical Overview.

In 1958 John Bowlby applied attachment theory to an understanding of the child's relationship to his mother. In his survey of existing research, Bowlby reported two revolutionary, albeit simple, findings: (1) the infant's need for his parent is analogous to his need for food and (2) significant separation from or loss of the parent results in psychological trauma to the child. As we will see in later chapters, the trauma's effect on the child may range from minor, short-term emotional insecurities to major, long-lasting aberrations in the ability to relate to other human beings. (As illustrated by the case of Candy above, many foster children have experienced chronic interruptions in the relationship to their caretakers. Indeed, attachment-disordered foster children have often suffered countless, painful disruptions in their earliest years, which may scar them emotionally for life.)

Drawing heavily from "instinct theory" and its notions about "imprinting," Bowlby's work culminated in a detailed account of the infant's growing connection, i.e. attachment, to his caretaker (Bowlby, 1969). His innovative notions about infant attachment spurred others to examine attachment in the laboratory setting, in the delivery room, in the pediatric clinic, and in the psychotherapist's office (see Ainsworth, 1978; Pound, 1982; Brazelton, 1990; Cline, 1979; Magid, 1987; Fahlberg, 1979; Belsky and Nezworski, 1988; and Greenberg, Cicchetti and Cummings, 1990). Today, Bowlby's thoughts are tremendously useful in the understanding and treatment of abused and neglected foster children, whose attachments to others have been severely damaged through repeated exposure to separation from and loss of the parents or to mistreatment, rejection and abandonment by them.

A Definition of Attachment.

Broadly speaking, attachment may be defined as a "lasting psychological connectedness between human beings." In the psychological study of children, more specifically, attachment is the emotional bond which grows between the child and parent and vice versa. Despite an almost magical, tender quality ascribed to attachment, it remains a hypothetical construct. That is, attachment is essentially an abstraction—an unseen internal state in the child and parent (Bowlby, 1969; Ainsworth, 1978; Mahler, 1975).

The Survival Value of Attachment.

In humans, as with other mammals, offspring attachment to its caretaker (e.g. mother) improves the chances for survival (Bowlby, 1973). By keeping the immature, helpless infant/child close, the caretaker reduces risks to the child's health and safety. In turn, by encouraging the caretaker to remain close by, the infant/child contributes to his own survival. The normally attached child, for example, by remaining relatively close to his caretaker, escapes many hazards which beset attachment-disordered children, such as running into busy streets, walking off with strangers, getting into poisonous substances, and the like.

In addition to physical survival, the child's psychological well-being is predicated on secure attachment formation. Indeed, children who lack secure attachment evidence behavioral and emotional problems of various levels of severity. As we will see later in the book, traumatized foster children often suffer from abnormal attachments, out of which spring a variety of complex emotional and behavioral problems.

Attachment behaviors in the normal child emerge very clearly in specific critical situations, such as: when the child is sick, tired, or injured; in the presence of a stranger or strange surroundings; and when the child is left alone (i.e. separated from the parent). (See Table 1.1 for a summary of critical situations which elicit attachment behaviors in the infant/child.) To reiterate, increases in the child's attachment behaviors in critical situations serve a survival value, keeping the parent and child closest when the child is most vulnerable. These situations evoke a strong feeling of anxiety in the child, who reacts by increasing attachment behaviors (see below), such as crying or seeking out the parent for comfort or protection.

As we will see later in this book, attachment-disordered foster children do not act as expected in critical situations. Many of them do not come to the foster parent (or any other caretaker) when they are sick, injured, or frightened. In fact, these disturbed children often avoid the caretakers in critical situations, preferring to handle the crises themselves. Undoubtedly related to their history of mistreatment by adults, these children learn to fend for themselves.

| *Critical Situations Which Elicit Attachment-Behaviors* | •Illness
•Unavailability of Caretaker
•Presence of Stranger
•Aloneness
•Darkness
•Novel Settings
•Injury
•Danger
•Hunger
•Fatigue
(From Bowlby, 1973) | **Table 1.1** |

Infant/Child Attachment Behaviors.

Child attachment behaviors are observable actions which point to underlying attachment. Attachment behaviors in the child serve to keep the caretaker close by, in physical contact with, and/or otherwise connected to the child. These behaviors of the infant/child towards the caretaker change with age, but include the following: making eye contact with, smiling at, crying, pouting, protesting angrily, searching after, following, reaching for, signaling to, clinging or holding onto, seeking to be picked up, and sitting with. (See Table 1.2 below for infant attachment behaviors.) These behaviors from the child serve to promote and sustain contact with or proximity to the parent (Ainsworth, 1978). Their purpose is, in effect, to reward the parent for staying close and to punish the parent for moving away. As the child becomes more verbal, speech increasingly replaces some of these earlier primitive, physical forms of engagement between parent and offspring (Mahler, 1975). However, any experienced foster parent knows that older, disturbed foster children resort to highly primitive forms of attachment behavior. Insatiably needy foster children, for example, who seem to be constantly clinging to the foster parent, continue to show the more primitive attachment behaviors usually seen in infants/toddlers. These clingy foster children, from an attachment formation standpoint, are developmentally arrested.

Infant/Child Attachment Behavior	•Eye Contact •Smiling •Pouting •Protesting Separation •Following •Searching •Reaching •Signaling or calling to •Holding or clinging •Seeking to be picked up •Sitting with	Table 1.2

The Parent or Caretaker's Role in Attachment.

The child's attachment cannot be understood outside the context of his relationship to attachment figures, i.e. his parents or chief caretakers. Indeed, infant attachment develops, not in a vacuum, but in interaction. It is important, then, to consider the parents' role in attachment formation.

In a nutshell, development of secure attachment in the infant is strongly influenced by two caretaker qualities: accessibility and responsiveness (see Table 1.3). Accessibility means that the parent is present and available, physically and emotionally, to the infant and child. That is, the attachment figure is with the infant/child throughout the period of attachment. Indeed, secure attachment requires the presence of a figure to whom one becomes attached.

Two Essential Caretaker Qualities	•**Responsiveness** •**Accessibility**	**Table 1.3**

By parental responsiveness is meant that the caretaker sensitively, accurately and directly addresses the child's needs. The responsive attachment figure can accurately read signals from the infant/child and can anticipate needs based on past experience with her young child. She successfully identifies the child's needs from cries, facial expressions, vocalizations, body language, and overt behavior. Depending upon the stage of attachment and the specific child, the parent's response differs. For example, during the "pre-attachment" stage (see ahead), the parent feeds, diapers, comforts, holds, and stimulates the infant, when the need is expressed. Later, during the "active attachment" stage the caretaker remains at times more physically distant, though emotionally available to the child. During this stage, the caretaker must tolerate and encourage independence, while providing the child a "secure base" through her emotional availability (Bowlby, 1969; Mahler, 1975).

Inevitably, if the caretaker is accessible and responsive to the infant/child, attachment will form (given a normal infant/child). However, "responsiveness and accessibility" must span the first three to five years of the child's life for attachment to mature and solidify. It is important to note here that normal infants and young children usually are quite receptive to caretakers. They, figuratively speaking, "soak up" as much parenting, nurturing, and stimulation as possible. The disturbed, attachment-disordered foster child, however, is another story. This unfortunate child often rejects nurturing behavior from the accessible and reliable foster parents due to his past history of maltreatment from caretakers. As we will see in later chapters, the foster child's jaundiced view of parent figures can contaminate his relationship to the foster parents. A substantial portion of this book will address treatment approaches which can change the child's view and allow him to accept caretaking from the foster parents.

Stages of Normal Attachment Formation.

The birth of the child and the birth of attachment are not simultaneous (Mahler, 1975). While physical birth of the infant occurs with a sudden, remarkable event, attachment emerges over time and through a series of comparatively gradual stages. As shown in Table 1.4 below, attachment to the caretaker has been found to develop across four predictable stages during the critical period of his first three to five years of life (see Bowlby, 1973; Ainsworth, 1978; Mahler, 1975).

(Note: The formation of attachment during the first years of life is critical to later psychological health. As we will see ahead, in those children who have failed to attach during a "window of opportunity" in the first five years of life, the chances for developing normal attachment relationships later in life is diminished.)

In the first stage of normal attachment formation—the"pre-attachment" stage (Ainsworth, 1978)—the tiny infant (birth to three months old) is totally dependent upon the caretaker, who reacts to the child protectively. The infant, though totally dependent, is not completely inert in the attachment interaction. He orients towards the sound of the female voice; he tracks moving objects with his eyes; and he reflexively reaches out to be held. At this first stage, his smile is relatively indiscriminate and reflexive; and on the whole, he is a comparatively passive player in the attachment drama.

Next, in the "recognition/discrimination," stage (Ainsworth, 1978; Bowlby, 1969) the infant (age three to eight months) differentiates visually between his primary caretaker and others; in her presence he vocalizes differently and cries in a distinct fashion when she leaves the room. He examines his primary caretaker enthusiastically and smiles at and "greets" her after brief separations.

In the "active attachment" stage, from eight months to three years of age, the child shows clear preference for the primary caretaker (Ainsworth, 1978; Bowlby, 1969). Correspondingly, the child shows a "stranger reaction," which indicates he clearly discriminates between his primary attachment figure and strangers. At this stage also, the child checks back to the caretaker's face, visually touching base with her. In addition, the child crawls (or walks) away from his caretaker. He becomes intoxicated by his newfound mobility and begins to explore the world outside his immediate attachment relationship, (i.e. he "practices" separating (Mahler, 1975).) The toddler at this stage revels in his

Table 1.4

Stages in Attachment Formation

Age	Stage	Description
Birth- 3 months	Pre-attachment	Infant orients towards the sound of the caretaker'svoice; he tracks visually. Infant smiles reflexively.
3-8 months	Recognition/ Discrimination	Infant differentiates between primary caretaker and others. Smiles are based on recognition. Infant scans the caretaker's face with excitement. Infant greets caretaker and vocalizes differently to her.
8-36 months	Active Attachment	Stranger reaction emerges. Infant shows clear preference for the chief caretaker. He checks back to his caretaker's face. Child crawls or walks away from caretaker. Child explores without anxiety. Child acts intermittently in dependent and then independent ways.
36 months-	Partnership	Attachment solidifies. Child shows increased ability to communicate needs verbally. Child negotiates differences.

exploration, independence and locomotion, relatively unconcerned about his mother's whereabouts.

During the later half of this stage (i.e. from eighteen to thirty-six months of age) the child oscillates between desire for independence and yearning for dependence (Mahler, 1975). Much more ambivalent about exploration, the child seeks to periodically reunite with the mother and remains aware of her presence or absence. At this stage the child "refuels" with the caretaker by running to her for hugs, calling to her for attention from afar, and looking in her direction for an approving glance (Mahler, 1975). Temporarily refueled, the child can then return to confident exploration until such time as his "fuel" runs low; then he reunites for refueling once again. By this stage in attachment formation, the child has become a much more active, more sophisticated player in the attachment relationship (Cicchetti, Cummings, Greenberg, and Marvin, 1990). Verbal interchanges and "distance contact" between the child and caretaker may increasingly replace physical contact, proximity seeking, and other more primitive attachment behaviors.

In the "partnership" stage (i.e. thirty-six months and beyond), the child solidifies attachment relationships and becomes further sophisticated in the verbal communication of needs and in the verbal negotiation of differences with his caretakers (Bowlby, 1969; Ainsworth, 1978; Speltz, 1990). (As we will see ahead, many disturbed foster children never reach the partnership stage nor have they mastered the skill of communicating their needs and of negotiating conflicts and differences with caretakers.)

The Securely Attached Child and the "Internal Working Model."

The stages of attachment formation outlined above follow sequentially, if the interrelationship between caretaker and child remains unbroken, secure and healthy. Thus, the typical infant/child, having found his primary attachment figure both accessible and responsive to him, develops a secure attachment. This attachment provides a sound footing upon which the structure of personality is built.

On average, by the "partnership stage," the attached child has developed a positive "internal working model" (Bowlby, 1969;), i.e. an optimistic expectation, mental representation, or "blueprint" regarding himself, his caretaker, and their relationship. (As discussed in later chapters, the disturbed foster child often has developed a pessimistic, cynical "negative working model" of himself and his caretakers which interferes with his development of healthy attachment relationships in the foster family.)

In the normal, securely attached child, the working model would contain mostly positive images of himself and his caretakers. Table 1.5 outlines the working model of a normal, well-attached child.

The Positive Working Model	About himself:
	1. I am worthwhile/wanted.
	2. I am safe.
	3. I am capable.
	About caretakers:
	1. They are available.
	2. They are responsive.
	3. They meet my needs.

Table 1.5

The securely attached young child has developed, what has been called by others, "basic trust" (Erikson, 1968), an expectation that the world will be generally safe and that close relationships will be satisfying. Furthermore, he is secure in himself and in his relationships to primary attachment figures; he knows that he belongs and to whom he belongs (Bowlby, 1969). With that comes a sense of inner tranquility, which permits greater independence and the ability to attend to his own needs confidently. Relatively unconcerned about the most important relationships in his close-in, "proximate world," this child can venture out into the "distal" world-at-large. That is, he can become thoroughly absorbed in play, learning and mastery of the world around him without inordinate fears about loss of his parents. The normally attached child also has a well-formed conscience, a sense of right and wrong which grows out of his desire to please his attachment figures. He shows need awareness, a range of genuine emotion, and the ability to identify and express needs in a remarkably insightful fashion; and he displays affection and anger freely. In all, this child relates emphatically to children and adults, and he can negotiate disagreements through increasingly complex verbal interchanges (Ainsworth, 1978).

Reaction to Disruption in the Attachment Relationship.

Although minor disruptions in the caretaker-child relationship are common and often harmless, major separations from and losses of the caretaker can disrupt the child's attachment in very destructive ways. Major disruptions to attachment may occur in cases of parent mental or physical illness and/or death; abandonment of the child by the parent; chronic abuse, neglect, or exploitation of the child; and periodic rejection of the child (Magid, 1987; Fraiberg, 1980; Main and Solomon, 1990; Main and Hesse, 1990). Importantly, certain infant/child factors can also precipitate disruptions in the growing caretaker-child bond. For instance, prematurity, early life-threatening illnesses, and hyperactivity may negatively impact the continuity of the attachment relationship (Delaney, 1990; Brazelton and Cramer, 1990.)

Research has clearly demonstrated a distinct, three-part cycle (i.e. protest-despair-detachment) in the infant/toddler's response to disruptions in attachment i.e. during and after brief separation from the mother in a laboratory setting (Ainsworth, 1978) or in longer periods of separation due to, for example, lengthy hospitalization of the mother (Bowlby, 1973). This cycle in infants/toddlers can be used as a prototype for understanding reactions in older foster children who have experienced significant separations and losses.

| *Reaction to Disruption in Attachment* | The Protest-Despair-Detachment Cycle:

Protest — Crying, distress, pursuit of the mother, searching after the mother, temper tantruming.

Despair — Depression, quiet withdrawal, refusal to be comforted by the stranger, disinterest in play or exploration.

Detachment — Lack of interaction with the primary caretaker after reunion, active avoidance of the caretaker, and failure to recognize the caretaker. | **Table 1.6** |

The protest-despair-detachment cycle is predictable (see Table 1.6). Upon first becoming aware of his caretaker's absence, the child initially protests; that is, he cries, whines, calls to, pursues, searches after, rages, and/or otherwise makes his displeasure known. Finding that his protests are lodged in vain and that his attempts to get his caretaker to return are futile, the child might despair, i.e. become saddened, depressed, and lethargic. He refuses the stranger's attempts at comforting him. Thirdly, the child eventually detaches from others in a withdrawn, somewhat cynical posture. Even if reunited with the caretaker, the child may rebuff her, fail to recognize her, and remain remarkably disinterested in becoming involved with her again. (Mothers and fathers of infants/toddlers/preschoolers often observe the protest-despair-detachment cycle at the babysitter's or nursery school. When the parents come to pick up the child they are told the child cried (protest) for a half hour after they dropped him off. They are further told that the child was inconsolate (despair) for a long period of the day, retreating into himself and refusing contact with the babysitter. When the parents attempt to engage the child at the end of the day, he may appear aloof, disinterested in them, and may even refuse to leave the nursery (detachment).)

A grasp of the protest-despair-detachment cycle in normal children can foster an understanding of serious attachment problems (in children of all ages) caused by chronic separation and loss. The three-part cycle, when repeated frequently during the first three years of life may result in short and long-term aberrations in attachment formation. Indeed, depending upon the chronicity and severity of caretaker-child disruptions (and perhaps upon the child's innate temperament and age at time of disruption), attachment becomes weakened, seriously damaged, and abnormal.

Abnormal Attachments.

When the infant/child fails to develop a secure relationship to a chief caretaker, abnormal attachment results (Ainsworth, 1968; Main and Solomon, 1990). Of the four patterns of attachment—Types A, B, C, and D—which have been found in infants and young children, three are abnormal. Researchers have discovered, using so-called "separation experiments," that the normally or securely attached (Type B) infant, after brief periods of physical separation from his caretaker, shows clear signs of missing her; then, upon reunion with her, the Type B infant seeks and finds closeness to her and, as a result seems to be secure enough to eventually resume play or exploration. One could say that this child shows protest but does not despair or detach. This is not the case, as we will see next, with the other patterns of attachment.)

The three patterns of abnormal attachment include the following: (1) Type A — insecure-avoidant; (2) Type C — insecure-ambivalent; and (3) Type D — disorganized/disoriented (Ainsworth, 1978; Main and Solomon, 1990; Main and Hesse, 1990). These patterns (see Table 1.7) first identified in infants, appear to show some permanence over time as children mature. That is, avoidant children tend to remain avoidantly attached, while disorganized children remain that way in follow-up studies. (It seems likely that all three patterns of abnormal attachment are observed in maltreated children who are subjected to a great deal of disruption during attachment formation years. After placement in foster care, many of these children remain insecure or disorganized in their attachments. In the worst cases, these children are highly resistant to change.)

For clarity's sake, we will briefly describe the three abnormal attachment patterns as they emerge in the "separation experiments."

(1) Insecure-avoidant (Type A) infants casually avoid and nonchalantly ignore the caretaker after being reunited with her. These "Type A" infants/young children appear to avoid closeness to or interaction with the mother after reunion with her, although not in an extremely angry or actively rejecting way. They might merely move away, glance away, or fail to cling to their mothers, and they treat a stranger much like they treat the mother. Insecure-avoidant infants ironically may show little distress during the separation period away from the mother (Ainsworth, 1978). These children might be seen as relatively detached.

Three Patterns of Abnormal Attachment	**Type A —** Insecure-avoidant **Type C —** Insecure-ambivalent **Type D —** Disorganized-disoriented	**Table 1.7**

(2) Infants with insecure-ambivalent (Type C) attachments are markedly distressed during separation and upon reunion are inconsolable, obsessed with the parent, and vacillate between need for closeness with and anger at the parent (Ainsworth, 1978; Main and Hesse, 1990). These infants/young children show angry dependency mixed with active and/or passive resistance to closeness to and contact with the mother. Insecure-ambivalent infants/children are very distressed during the period of separation from the mother. These children would not be seen as detached, but rather as highly protesting.

(3) Of all three abnormal attachment patterns, the disorganized/disoriented (Type D) infant shows the most confusing, contradictory attachment behavior. His behavior is marked by two conflicting drives: one to approach and the other to flee the caretaker. The infant may show a burst of angry behavior followed by sudden "freezing," or "dazed behavior" (Main and Solomon, 1990). This behavior might be akin to that described by Fraiberg (1980) as "frozen watchfulness" in maltreated children. After being reunited, the disorganized/disoriented infant might sit on parent's lap but with eyes averted, or might allow the parent to hold him but with his limbs stiff. A particularly curious example of such contradictory behavior is that of the child who smiles

obviously but fearfully. Other behaviors which signal disorganized/disoriented attachment in the infant are: infant goes away from or fails to seek out the caretaker when distressed or frightened; infant attempts to leave with a stranger rather than staying with the caretaker; and infant shows fright at the sight of the caretaker after reunion (Main and Solomon, 1990). It is likely that Type D infants have experienced a great deal of trauma in the relationship to their attachment figures. They show an unusual form of detachment.

Concluding Remarks.

Attachment between infant and caretaker is prerequisite to physical survival and emotional health of the child. Typically, an infant/child marches through four predictable stages of development on the road to secure, mature attachment. When the process of attachment unfolds without significant disruptions, the child becomes normally, securely attached, as seen in his positive "internal working model," conscience development, the ability to empathize, a sense of basic trust in the world, an inner feeling of security, a growing awareness of his needs, the capacity to express affection and anger directly, and the learning of negotiating skills. However, when significant disruptions mar the attachment process, a pattern of abnormal attachment may emerge. In the case of the maltreated child, the development of an abnormal attachment is highly likely, although not inevitable (Anthony, 1987).

In the next chapter, focus will turn to how the attachment-disordered, maltreated child has developed a negative "working model," e.g. a mental snapshot, of himself and his caretakers which relates to the conduct problems he manifests in foster home placement.

2 | The Attachment-Disordered Foster Child

A large share of children who have been chronically abused and neglected ultimately develop full-blown attachment disorders. Many of these children are eventually placed in foster homes, where these disorders are displayed in living color. In this chapter focus turns to attachment disorders in foster children and to the abusive/neglectful early histories which cause them. Also, discussion will center on the conduct problems which are symptomatic of attachment-disorders and which relate to the disturbed child's distorted view of the world. But, before addressing these issues, consider the three following cases of attachment-disordered foster children.

Case Studies.

Jimmy, age eight, was a terribly abused and neglected boy, who had been raised by his cruel older brothers, due to the frequent absence of his alcoholic mother from the home. By second grade, Jimmy had spent more time living with foster families, of which there had been several, than with his birth family. Although Jimmy had problems in the present foster home with lying, stealing, and fire-setting, it was his violence towards the younger foster children and Barney — the foster family dog — which was most alarming. Whenever Jimmy was left alone with the other children, even for a moment, someone "accidentally" got hurt. A recently placed infant foster child automatically cried, whenever Jimmy even walked into the room. The family dog, a sloe-eyed retriever, had patiently endured minor abuse from a host of foster children over the years. However, none of it had prepared him for the calculated, cruel mistreatment he received from Jimmy. On two occasions Jimmy attempted unsuccessfully to push the harmless dog off the second floor balcony. Several times, Jimmy deliberately threw the tennis ball into the busy street for the dog to fetch. Miraculously, Barney survived the balcony, speeding traffic... and Jimmy.

* * * * *

Bobby was a lifeless, lukewarm sort of boy who blended almost invisibly into the foster home. Though he had been placed there for almost a year, Bobby was a "phantom child" to the foster parents. A boy who had spent many of his seven years in abject poverty, both economic and psychological, he rarely smiled and never laughed. Bobby answered questions monosyllabically. At the community swimming pool, he waded to an unpopulated corner away from the splashing, noise, and fun. On the rare occasions when he hurt himself, Bobby failed to cry or seek out comfort. His dentist discovered that Bobby had an abscessed tooth which should have caused the most excruciating pain. The foster mother never knew about it, because Bobby had never once mentioned it. At bedtime, Bobby tolerated a hug and a kiss. However, he never approached his foster parents, and in fact, drifted away as soon as he could.

* * * * *

Sally was not an easy child to like, even after two years in a good foster home. This was the fifth foster home she had lived with, since she was first taken away from her maternal grandmother during infancy. The grandmother had been saddled with the responsibility of raising several grandchildren. A reluctant parent figure, the grandmother reared the children out of a dogged, joyless sense of duty. As a result, she gave Sally and the other children only minimal, custodial care. When the task of raising her grandchildren became overwhelming, she periodically turned the children over to the local welfare agency for a few months. As the children grew older, their behavior problems escalated to the point that grandmother could no longer tolerate them. Eventually, she did not want them back from the foster home and refused to even visit them.

By her fifth out-of-home placement, Sally was quite unlovable. The foster parents reported that she made it nearly impossible for them to get close to her — to attach to her. When they felt things were going smoothly, Sally inevitably undermined progress. Just when the foster parents felt they could trust her, Sally would revert to stealing and lying. Her smoldering anger lay unverbalized but just under the surface at all times. Once, to spite the foster parents, Sally destroyed the pretty dress they bought her for her tenth birthday. The foster parents described her as deeply controlling and resisting any adult authority in a passive-resistant way. For example, when sent to her room for misbehavior,

Sally would remain there for hours after she was told that she could come out; this seemed to be her attempt to remain "one up" and in control, even when punished. Sally blamed the foster parents for conspiring with the caseworker to prevent visits with her grandmother. Ironically, she held her grandmother blameless for placing her outside the home.

* * * * *

The cases of Jimmy, Bobby, and Sally above highlight five issues to be addressed in this chapter:

1. What attachment disorders are and how they are manifested in foster children;

2. The causes of attachment disorders in foster children;

3. The negative "working model" which the abused and neglected child has developed regarding himself and caretakers;

4. The failure of attachment-disordered children to identify their feelings and to negotiate their wants and desires with their caretakers;

5. The relationship between conduct or behavior problems and the above four issues.

Attachment Disorders and Their Symptoms.

Jimmy, Bobby, and Sally each suffer from an attachment disorder related to his/her early history of abuse and neglect. An attachment disorder is a serious, relatively fixed emotional and behavioral disturbance in the child, whose early attachment relationships were abnormal. Indeed, the foster child correctly diagnosed as attachment-disordered is often a deeply disturbed child with aberrant behavior. Simply put, he is an emotional misfit — a child who has been exposed to destructive factors early in life which have damaged his sense of security and his trust in caretakers. Exposed to many disruptions during the earliest years, many maltreated foster children develop a negative picture of people which influences all later relationships.

Attachment disorders may underlie many clinical diagnoses which have been used traditionally to label extremely troubled foster children — diagnoses such as: reactive attachment disorder of infancy, conduct disorder, autistic disorder, oppositional defiant disorder, separation anxiety disorder, avoidant disorder, overanxious disorder, and identity disorder (DSM III-R, 1987). Though the exact connection between early patterns of abnormal attachment (i.e. Type A, C, or D) and later diagnoses remains unknown, the vestiges of early maltreatment and related attachment problems remain highly measurable in older, disturbed foster children; some of these children are thought to be "insecurely attached," "avoidant," or "unattached" (Magid and McKelvey, 1987;

Symptoms	**Category & Examples**
of the	**Sadism/violence**
Attachment-	cruelty to animals and
Disordered	children; vandalism
Child	destructiveness; assaultive
	behavior; self-injurious
	behavior; firesetting
	Disordered eating
	stealing and hoarding food;
	gorging; food refusal
	Counterfeit emotionality
	theatrical display; superficial
	charm; emotional radar;
	indiscriminate attachment
	Kleptomania/compulsive lying
	chronic stealing; pathological
	lying
	Sexual obsessions
	seductive behavior or clothing;
	sexual activity with other
	children; bestiality
	Passive-aggression
	face-to-face compliance;
	refusal to answer questions;
	provoking anger in others;
	wetting and soiling
	Defective conscience
	absence of guilt; denial and
	projection of blame

(See Cline, 1979; Magid and McKelvey, 1987; and Delaney, 1990.)

Table 2.1

Cline, 1979; Delaney, 1990).

Although attachment disorders can take many shapes, in this book we will only address the attachment disorder which most closely resembles the "conduct-disordered" (see the DSM III-R) or the "unattached" child (Magid and McKelvey, 1987; Cline, 1979; Delaney, 1990). Thus, from this point forward in the book, "attachment-disordered" will indicate a conduct-disordered or "unattached" child with a serious underlying attachment disorder. Table 2.1 lists the common symptoms of the attachment-disordered foster child. This child may display a broad spectrum of behavior problems, ranging from sadistic cruelty to animals to self-injury; from firesetting to lying and stealing; from gorging of food to refusal to eat; and from sexual precocity to bedwetting. While these symptoms are diverse, they cluster into seven main categories: sadism/violence; disordered eating; counterfeit emotionality; kleptomania/compulsive lying; sexual obsessions; passive-aggression; and defective conscience.

Those who live and work with troubled foster children will quickly recognize many, if not all, of the symptoms or conduct problems seen in Table 2.1. These symptoms may vary with the age of the child and the severity of his attachment disorder (see Appendix for detailed descriptions and examples of conduct problems and symptoms of the attachment-disordered child). Later in this chapter we will discuss the significance of the conduct problems which are symptomatic of attachment disorders. But first some thoughts about causes of attachment disorders.

Causes of Attachment Disorders.

The cause of the maltreated child's attachment disorder has been assumed to be inadequate, hostile, or abusive caretaking (Spieker and Booth, 1988; Crittendon, 1988; Speltz, 1990). The histories of many disturbed foster children are rife with deficient caretaking, as in the following case studies:

* * * * *

Joey, age five, unfortunately resembled his biological father, who had been mercilessly battering of Joey's mother. A woman who had also been sexually abused by her father and older brothers, she had never felt close to Joey — a representative of the abusing male world. As an infant, she handled Joey roughly, yanking him around by the arm, which she ultimately fractured. Joey was not well cared for, and was left in rags while his sisters were "dolled up." Johnny was frequently brought to the emergency room for injuries, as he was "accident prone" and reckless.

* * * * *

Cindy, a seven-year-old girl with slumped posture and expressionless eyes, sauntered into the room where she was to have a supervised visit with her parents. A malodorous, unkempt, low-functioning couple, her birth parents showed no excitement when they were reunited with Cindy. During the visit the parents mechanically asked a litany of prepared questions, which Cindy answered without elaboration. The case record showed that Cindy had been taken from the parents by the welfare agency on a dozen or more occasions due to neglect, malnourishment, failure to take Cindy to the doctor, and lack of supervision. Cindy at times during the session tried to take a parental role towards her mother and father.

* * * * *

In play, Bart, an angry three-year-old, only knew how to pound on, tear up, and eventually destroy toys. History revealed that Bart had been repeatedly abandoned by his birth mother, when she would run off with boyfriends. Bart was left with a countless number of babysitters, relatives, friends, and even strangers. Indeed, Bart seemed to be as comfortable with a stranger as he was with his mother.

* * * * *

While some maltreated children may be "invulnerable" to the effects of abuse, undoubtedly the lion's share of victimized children develop some attachment disorders of a relatively fixed nature (Anthony, 1987; Greenberg and Speltz, 1988). They are subjected to many separations from and losses of the primary caretakers. Most probably they have cycled through the protest-despair-detachment sequence innumerable times. During infancy, many of these children may form insecure, resistant, ambivalent, or disorganized/disoriented (Type A, C, or D) attachment patterns due to the insensitivity, unresponsiveness, unreliability, and unavailability of their caretakers (Bowlby, 1973; Brazleton, 1990). By the age of two or three, these children may already be developing full-blown attachment disorders.

Though chronically angry, these attachment-disordered children are often unwilling or unable to directly express anger to their caretakers (Delaney, 1990). Fearful of abusive retaliation or outright rejection or abandonment by their caretakers, these children must curtail direct expression of frustration. Indeed, many of the conduct problems of the maltreated child provide an outlet, however indirect, for pent-up, often unconscious, aggressive feelings towards caretakers. As we will see ahead, it is often in the foster family that anger emerges, though often indirectly, with a negative effect on the placement.

The Negative Working Model.

As explained in Chapter One, the "working model" is the cognitive snapshot, mental representation, or psychic image that the child forms about himself, his caretakers, and their relationship to him (see Bowlby, 1969; 1973). This working model emerges out of a myriad of interactions with the caretaker, and by the age of twelve months infants already show clear individual differences in working models, although they cannot yet verbalize about it (Schneider-Rosen, 1990). However, by three years of age the contents of the working model can be ascertained by analyzing children's verbalizations (Bretherton, Ridgeway, and Cassidy, 1990); and by four years of age, the working model may already be relatively fixed and resistant to change (Greenberg and Speltz, 1988). Generally speaking the working model stores overall impressions of accumulated experiences the child has had with his primary caretakers (Bretherton et al. 1990). More impressionistic than exact, the working model is an inner reflection of outer realities. As seen above, in the normal, securely attached child, the working model would contain a preponderance of positive images of self, caretakers, and their relationship.

It is important to note that a sizeable portion of the working model, once developed, appears to function at an unconscious level (Bowlby, 1969; 1973; Cicchetti, 1990). This may be explained by the fact that much of that psychic image is formed when the child is young and preverbal. The unconscious functioning of the working model is especially evident in the maltreated child, who often holds highly idealized, Pollyanna, conscious notions regarding his abusive, maltreating caretakers (e.g. his birth parents). At the same time, at an unconscious level, the maltreated child has developed cynical, pessimistic expectations about himself, caretakers, and the world. Consciously, for example, the foster child may hold these thoughts: "My mother loves me and looks after me," "My father is the best Dad a kid could have," and "My parents will visit me while I'm in foster care, because they love me." Simultaneously, at an unconscious level, the maltreated child holds different expectations — some too painful, confusing, frightening for the child to deal with. (For example, "My mother does not behave as if she wants me," "When my father hurts me, I feel terrified, helpless, and unwanted," and "When my parents fail to visit me, I feel rejected and angry.") For that reason negative aspects are reserved for the unconscious, where their presence is less visible but still felt. Indeed, as discussed ahead the unconscious, negative expectations of the troubled foster child dictate how he behaves, and how he stimulates others to behave towards him.

Many disturbed foster children develop a "negative working model." That is, the maltreated child's mental blueprint consists of highly negative expectations about caretakers and himself. As seen in Table 2.2 the maltreated child views himself as worthless, unsafe, and impotent to make an impact on others (Bretherton, 1990; Speltz, 1990). Simultaneously, he views caretakers as unreliable, unresponsive, and dangerous. He expects intimate relationships to be thoroughly undependable and ultimately frustrating of his needs. Though operating at an unconscious level, the negative working model has a dramatic influence on the child's behavior and on the maintenance of conduct problems. Indeed, the child who feels essentially worthless, unsafe, and impotent and who expects his caretakers to be unresponsive to his usual bids for attention, develops conduct problems which simultaneously assure some attention (albeit negative) and punish and distance the parent. Conduct problems stem directly from the negative, unconscious working model and relate to expectations about the self, the caretaker, and their relationship.

The Negative Working Model of the Maltreated Child	**About the Self:** 1. I am worthless. 2. I am unsafe. 3. I am impotent. **About the Caretaker:** 1. He/she is unresponsive. 2. He/she is unreliable. 3. He/she is threatening, dangerous, rejecting.	**Table 2.2**

As stated above, much of the negative working model remains at an unconscious level in the troubled foster child. Given his past, it may be less painful and/or more adaptive for the child to be unaware of the negative working model, since it might reduce potential, direct confrontation with a frightening individual. Maltreating caretakers may have used withdrawal of emotional supplies and support (Mahler, 1975; Masterson, 1972), ridicule (Speltz, 1990;), and other modes of punishment, threat, and intimidation to discourage any open display of protest from the child. This in effect relegates the negative working model to the realm of the unconscious. From a reinforcement point of view, verbalizations and thoughts about the negative aspects to the parent have been extinguished, leaving the child unaware of the "dark side" of the internal working model (Dollard and Miller, 1950).

Interestingly, representations and expectations arising out of the earliest relationships to the caretaker, may transfer to other, subsequent relationships. The child's working model is stubbornly resistant to change, so that if he learned to expect rejection, loss, insensitivity in the past, he continues to expect that in the present, even with different, sensitive, accepting, available caretakers (e.g. the foster parents). The working model becomes applied to these later relationships with adults and sometimes peers. In essence, the negative internal working model is unfairly superimposed upon any subsequent intimate relationships, though its relationship to the reality of the new relationship may be non-existent. (This "transference" phenomenon accounts for much trouble and disruption in the foster home and presents both challenges and opportunities in treatment of the maltreated foster child.) Indeed, in foster care the child's behavior reflects his working model and becomes a "reenactment" of the earlier, unsatisfying attachment relationships.

Failure to Negotiate with Caretakers.

The attachment-disordered foster child has never reached the stage of "partnership" with any caretaker. Along with that, this troubled child has never learned to identify clearly his feelings, to express them directly to his caretaker, and to negotiate differences or conflicts with her. Due to fear of the caretaker or to the expectation that his needs will not be met by her, the child fails to develop the ability to vocalize his thoughts, feelings, and needs. For him, it has been either dangerous or futile to do so in the past. In particular, it has been useless or hazardous for him to articulate his differences of opinion, his complaints, his anger, or opposing goals to his caretakers, as seen in the following two cases:

* * * * *

The foster mother described her preschool-aged foster daughter, Barbi, as a "little homemaker." Only four-years-old, Barbi made her bed without complaint, she picked up her toys after playing with them, and she never expressed any feelings of discontent. She was a "model child" to the extreme. According to the foster mother, Barbi had been completely potty trained by nine months of age. The oldest of three children, Barbi had become an assistant to the biological mother, who was depressed and withdrawn. Barbi was already able to diaper the younger two children and was often placed in charge of watching over them, while the birth mother napped on the couch. Barbi had been placed in foster care, after she had been found out front of the local grocery store at eleven P.M. She had been sent by her biological mother for a pack of cigarettes. When she was placed in the foster home, Barbi showed no distress at being separated from her mother, though she spoke of her younger two siblings. Barbi was extremely passive and meek with older children in the home, as well as with the foster parents. When children took her toys from her, she acquiesced without protest. However, when she was apparently angry at the foster parents, Barbi would sneak off and urinate in the corner of her bedroom.

When asked how she had raised Barbi to be so well-behaved, the birth mother stated, "You can't start young enough with kids...if you spoil them, they'll run all over you or want to be held all the time...if Barbi complained (as an infant) or cried, I popped her across the mouth — not real hard, mind you — she got the message. Now, all I have to do is raise my eyebrow at her and she won't even think about it (e.g. about getting angry)."

* * * * *

As you will recall from Chapter One, Candy had been placed in numerous foster homes before she was six-years-old. However, once placed in her ninth home — the therapeutic foster home — she stabilized somewhat, at least to the point where she was not asked to leave. Nonetheless, after a year in placement, Candy's problem behaviors still appeared intermittently. She continued to lie, steal, and urinate on the floors, and in general she withdrew from the foster family. Interestingly, Candy never confronted the foster parents directly, though she would argue incessantly with the other children in the home.

The foster mother gave an example of how overly compliant and non-assertive she was. On one occasion, Candy showed a highly uncharacteristic display of anger to the foster mother over use of the VCR. Candy, she explained, had a passion for specific videotaped cartoons and would watch them for hours. However, the other children in the home also had their favorite movies; thus, the foster parents set up a system whereby the children would take turns picking out what would be watched. The previous week, when the foster mother heard the children arguing about whose turn it was, she intervened somewhat hastily. In the process, she determined that it was another child's turn, not Candy's. In a rare instant of honest emotion, Candy protested loudly that it was her turn to watch her videotape. Over her protests, the foster mother stated, "If you are going to act that way, Candy, then you'll miss your next turn." In an almost eerie transformation, Candy immediately smiled and said compliantly, "Okay, Mom, I guess you're right." After that incident, however, Candy's behavior problems resurfaced suddenly, almost to the point they were at a year earlier.

* * * * *

As mentioned in Chapter One, attachment relationship between parents and child moves through predictable stages, if all goes right. When separations, losses, and maltreatment interfere with the proper unfolding of stages, children develop atypical attachment relationships to their caretakers. Children with attachment disorders, in particular, develop expectations about the treatment they will or will not receive from caretakers, and they act accordingly. Foster children with histories of serious maltreatment often fail to show the normal levels of direct, assertive expression of feelings, thoughts, and needs. Feeling unsafe, unwanted, and ineffective, they go "underground" with their desires, opinions, and complaints. Superficially compliant and pleasant and verbally unskilled at voicing needs and negotiating differences, they indirectly, behaviorally express themselves. This often results in conduct problems.

The Function of Conduct Problems.

As mentioned above, the maltreated, attachment-disordered foster child manifests a range of conduct problems usually related to dysfunction in the interpersonal sphere — more specifically to his inability to identify feelings and to negotiate differences with caretakers. From an attachment theory point of view, conduct problems serve three functions:

(1) to increase caretaker interactions, though they are likely to be negative, and potentially dangerous interactions (e.g.harsh punishment or abuse) (Speltz, 1990);

(2) to keep the caretaker at a distance physically/emotionally; and

(3) to vent pent-up frustration/anger.

The three functions, at times seemingly contradictory, underscore the insecurity-ambivalence-disorganization-disorientation of the attachment which the maltreated child has developed over time. It is likely, based on clinical observations, that attachment-disordered foster children are extremely ambivalent about caretaker involvement; they have anxieties about abuse and they are worried about loss, abandonment, and rejection.

The behavior that highly ambivalent children emit is confusing in that it serves simultaneously to bring the parent figure close and to keep him distant. It may also function to punish the parent, all the while it invites involvement. In effect, in foster placements, the disturbed child emotionally "handcuffs" the foster parents with these "mixed messages."

Maltreated, attachment-disordered foster children may accumulate and cling to a range of conduct problems which are quite provocative and passive-aggressive. Conduct problems include disruptive, habitually non-compliant, aggressive, and often out-of-control behaviors (Speltz, 1990). (See Appendix for detailed discussion of "symptoms" or conduct problems in attachment-disordered foster children.) Unfortunately, though the negative behaviors may be successful in evoking parental involvement, they may not improve or increase parental "sensitivity" (Speltz, 1990). In fact, the caretaker may be pressed by the child's behavior either into more disciplinarian, rejecting, angry parental behavior or at times into withdrawal from and rejection of the child. Indeed, conduct problems may render the child unmanageable, unlovable, and target for more abuse.

Ultimately, a vicious cycle ensues wherein the child's increasingly negative behavior evokes increasing parental involvement, but with a destructive impact to the attachment or relationship between caretaker and child (Speltz, 1990). In the foster care placement, the child may reenact or recreate old relationships with the surrogate parent figures (see Chapter Four). Eventually, the relationship between foster parent and child becomes more and more negative. Foster parents may even develop negative affect and abusive feelings towards the child. In time, the child may "spoil" the placement, and the foster parents may ask for the child to be removed from the home. Ironically, this outcome further validates the child's negative working model.

The obvious first question about the child's provocative, problem behaviors is: why would the child risk hazardous parental involvement through such negative behavior? The answer relates to the comments above regarding the threefold function of conduct problems: to increase caretaker behavior, to maintain a distance from the caretaker, and to vent frustration. The second question is: why does the maltreated child act provocatively even after he has been placed in a foster home wherein adequate caretaking is furnished to him? The probable answer is that the child remains insecure, avoidant, ambivalent, and disorganized in his attachment. Since he expects unavailability, rejection or maltreatment, his behavior reflects his unchanged negative expectations. His negative model forces him to continue to fend for himself and protect himself from the "abusive," uncaring adult world, all the while he attempts to exact from that world some measure of attention/nurturance.

Concluding Remarks.

The attachment-disordered foster child has often developed symptoms which would merit a diagnosis of "conduct disorder." These symptoms include lying, stealing, truancy, cruelty to animals, and other serious behavior problems. These significant behaviors emerge out of the foster child's negative working model, which is often unconscious and highly resistant to change. As we will see ahead, the negative working model may dictate how the child interacts (e.g. destructively) within the foster family. More specifically, the negative working model propels the child to interact in ways which simultaneously invite and reject foster parent involvement. Ultimately, the negative working model can bring about the demise of the foster placement, if left unrecognized and unaltered.

In the next chapter we turn to a discussion of reenactment, the recreation of old relationships with new individuals. We will see how the disturbed foster child seems compelled to recreate former, dysfunctional relationships which are in harmony with his negative working model. The meaning of conduct problems, which are often bewildering out of context, becomes clearer with an understanding of reenactment. Reenactment, likewise, makes greater sense when traced to the underlying negative working model.

3 | Reenactment

Many foster parents find themselves trapped in deja vu—unwitting prisoners of their foster child's past. They often become reluctant actors in a recurring drama written during the child's earliest years and replayed in their home. These foster parents undeservedly fall heir to their foster child's negative expectations—to his unresolved attachment issues.

The successful resolution of attachment issues in disturbed foster children depends upon impactful involvement by the foster parents (and psychotherapists, caseworkers, teachers, etc.) in altering the negative working model, i.e. his negative blueprint of the world. Without such alteration, the child's cynical picture of the world prompts him to isolate himself from those who might help him. Without major changes in how he views himself and caretakers, the child is "programmed" for failure and condemned to repeat the past—i.e. to reenact.

This chapter discusses reenactment and then proceeds to an explanation of the relationships between the negative working model, conduct problems, and reenactment.

Reenactment In Foster Care.

Reenactment, simply speaking, is defined as the recreation of old relationships with new people. (See Pearson, 1968 on topic of "transference.") Disturbed foster children often recreate destructive relationships in the foster placement; these relationships are based upon dysfunctional earlier interactions with unavailable, unresponsive, maltreating caretakers. Reenactment—this unhealthy recreation or reproduction—signals the presence of the underlying, negative working model of the maltreated child. The notion of reenactment gives meaning to the plethora of seemingly disjointed, at times confusing, conduct problems of the disturbed foster child. In short, conduct problems are merely familiar scenes from that recurrent drama.

With reenactment there is a "compulsive repetition" of history. That is, attachment-disordered children who are placed in foster families almost inevitably reenact the conflicts stemming from their earlier years. (Reenactment also occurs in adoptive, residential, and hospital placement.) Sadly, maltreated, attachment-disordered children, through reenactment, replay history in the present living situation with new individuals, to whom they assign old roles and expectations. The distorted perceptions, on-going conflicts, rigid roles and negative expectations are familiar and, oddly, comforting to these disturbed children, as seen in the case example below:

*   *   *   *   *

Without any honeymoon period at all, Steve started in with full-scale problem behaviors at school and in the foster home. Eleven-years-old, Steve would hide under his desk at school while making obscene noises. He ran out of the school house and shinnied up a tree, from which he threatened to jump. In the foster home, Steve kept things in a constant uproar. He encouraged the other foster children to run away from home with him on two separate occasions. He kept them up late, with giggling and silliness. He refused to listen to the foster mother at all and openly defied the foster father. Although he had many reasons to be angry about his out-of-home placement, Steve avoided any admission of anger. Instead, he appeared to provoke others to express anger for him or towards him. He refused to talk about it and in fact his behavior deteriorated sharply when his therapist confronted his underlying anger towards the placement.

*   *   *   *   *

In this case, Steve reenacted his earlier experiences of abandonment and rejection. He fully expected to be rejected by his present foster home, as he had by many homes before. Ironically, the offer of a home, a family, and a sense of belonging was more frightening than comforting to him. Indeed, the intimacy offered by a foster family is, to the disturbed foster child, a threat to an accustomed, cynical world in which there is neither hope nor disappointment. It is a threat also to a life in which one is expected (i.e. the negative working model) to survive, to fend for himself alone. Intimacy, attachment, love are misjudged to be attempts at manipulating or exploiting him. Attachment is associated with loss and let-down. In short, to the attachment-disordered child love is a Trojan Horse—a gift full of hidden dangers. (See Table 3.1 for a summary of reenactment.)

As will be shown ahead, treatment foster parents and the therapist must work together closely to expose and then to reduce reenactment—the mixture of reincarnated relationships, obsolete feelings, paranoid perceptions, self-destructive conflicts, conduct problems, and barriers to attachment.

Reenactment	**Recreates old relationships with new people.**
	Gives meaning to disjointed conduct problems.
	Signals an underlying negative working model.
	Presents barriers to attachment formation.
	May result in sabotage to the foster home placement.

Table 3.1

The Negative Working Model, Reenactment, and Conduct Problems.

In past chapters we have discussed the internal working model which children develop during the process of attachment formation. The "working model" can, in the best of situations (i.e. with normal attachment), contain positive expectations about the self, the world, and caretakers. We have also addressed the issue of the negative working model which evolves in the infant/child who has been maltreated (abused or neglected). Now, it is time to introduce the interrelationship between the negative working model, reenactment, and conduct problems. Table 3.2 presents a diagram of the cyclical relationship of the negative working model, conduct problems and reenactment.

As seen in the diagram, the negative working model contains, as it always does, expectations about the world which are bleak, cynical, and utterly negative. As mentioned earlier, the general premises of the negative working model are that caretakers are unresponsive, unreliable, and rejecting and that the self is worthless/unwanted, unsafe, and impotent to do anything about it. As the diagram indicates, conduct problems emerge out of these general premises or assumptions about the world. Conduct problems appear, sometimes in almost random, disjointed fashion and other times in predictable patterns. (In the so-called random category, for example, the child may be loving and well-behaved one day, and the next, may erupt, as if responding to random forces, with violence. On closer inspection, the forces at work may not be totally random. The child, for example, might be responding to a build up of grievances about which the foster parent had no clues. That is, all the while the child was smiling and compliant, he may have been stockpiling resentment, i.e. not telling the foster parent about what he needed or what offended him. In another case, the child might steal food, again almost at random, following a delightful, mutually rewarding day at the park with the foster mother. In this case, the child may undermine progress due to increased anxiety over intimacy.

On the other hand, with some conduct problems clearly predictable patterns may emerge. For example, the child might engage in power struggles on a daily basis with the foster parent over eating too slowly at the table. Or he might, like clockwork, act with cruelty to the family pet following any frustration he has encountered with the foster mother.)

Table 3.2

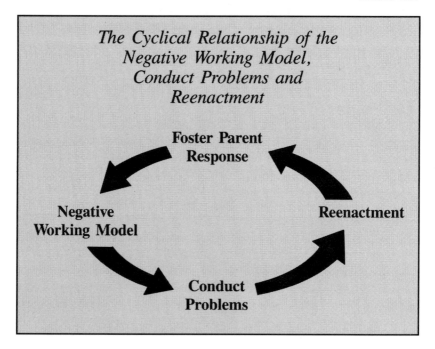

The Cyclical Relationship of the Negative Working Model, Conduct Problems and Reenactment

Foster Parent Response

Negative Working Model

Reenactment

Conduct Problems

Whether the conduct problems are totally disjointed and "random" in appearance, or predictably patterned, the net effect over time is that the child has begun to reenact his part of an earlier drama involving himself and his maltreating earlier caretakers. As you might expect, the child's reenactment of his side of earlier dysfunctional relationships often draws the foster parents into a response very similar to that of the maltreating parents. (We will discuss foster parents response (or countertransference) in the next chapter.) The reenactment and, most importantly, the resultant negative foster parent response, confirm the child's negative working model. Thus, a cyclical process develops here. The foster child's negative working model generates conduct problems; conduct problems in combination produce reenactment; reenactment invites negative responses from foster parents; and the negative responses confirm the child's negative working model. Then, the process repeats itself.

Now, we turn to some case studies which illustrate the interrelationship between the negative working model, conduct problems, and reenactment.

Case Studies.

"Boomer" was a slight, shorter than average eight-year-old Vietnamese boy who was placed with a treatment foster home after having failed with five regular foster families in two years. Abandoned as an infant by his single mother, reportedly a prostitute in South Viet Nam, Boomer was raised in a poorly funded orphanage until the age of five; then he was adopted by an American couple. Later it was discovered that Boomer had suffered horrendous neglect, was malnourished for several years, and received inadequate nurturing, affection, stimulation, and protection from adult staff in the orphanage. Additionally, he was a victim of both cruel physical and periodic sexual abuse in the orphanage, having been exploited by older boys and possibly by some aberrant staff member.

Years later, when Boomer began sexually acting-out with the family dog, his then adoptive parents asked for removal from the home. Of course, earlier in the placement Boomer had shown other conduct problems: constant lying, shallow relating, unending, meaningless chatter with the foster mother, soiling and smearing of feces, stealing and stockpiling food in his room, and provoking other children to abuse him both physically and sexually. Six-years-old at the time of his removal from the adoptive family, Boomer was placed in one foster home after another, until he arrived in treatment foster care. By then his already serious attachment problems had been exacerbated by "foster care drift," that is, by his odyssey through the foster care system. His behavior by the sixth placement following adoption was unmistakably more pathological. Most of his escalating behavior problems were marked by an underlying negative working model. He became skilled at sabotaging placements in quick fashion and had an uncanny ability to identify what he needed to do to elicit mistreatment, abusive feelings, and rejection from others. With his conduct problems he eventually reenacted themes of rejection, loss, mistreatment from his earliest years. As a result, Boomer undermined each placement in turn. He had become expert at identifying, most likely at an unconscious level, what he needed to do to sabotage each specific placement. For example, with the religious foster family, he refused to go to church, made up a filthy version of the dinner prayer which he taught the other children, and used pages from the family Bible to wipe himself. With one fastidious foster family, Boomer gradually became messier, refused to take out the garbage, and hid dirty dishes in the cupboards. He would sit in his room all day as punishment, rather than clean it up as requested.

In each of the failed foster home placements, the parents confessed their feelings of unsettling rage and confusion about the placement. They each reported a sense that they were not allowed by Boomer to love him and care for him. Gradually, they felt like abandoning him, though they each had vowed not to let that happen. In each case, it seemed to them that Boomer had forced them into the role of rejecting him.

* * * * *

The attachment-disordered child's distorted view of the world and expectation of mistreatment do not simply disappear upon placement into a benign, responsive foster home. Indeed, the attachment-disordered child clings stubbornly to his negative working model about caretakers and about himself, and he transfers the contents of that model, i.e. feelings, perceptions and expectations, onto the undeserving foster family.

In the case of Boomer, the cyclical relationship of negative working model, conduct problems, and reenactment seem clear. In brief, Boomer's negative working model contained negative expectations which were derived from his history of early loss, abandonment, mistreatment, neglect and deprivation, and sexual exploitation. These expectations were that caretakers were cruel, rejecting, unpredictable, ungiving, harsh, heartless, and unavailable. Boomer's view of himself was that he was unwanted/worthless, unsafe, and impotent. (Feelings of deep depression and unending rage would also be associated with this child's view of himself and his caretakers.) Out of the negative working model (and the depression and rage) emerged the many, seemingly disjointed conduct problems named above: stealing, lying, provoking others to anger, etc. Indeed, though unconscious, the negative working model dictated much of Boomer's dysfuntional, maladaptive behavior.

As the conduct problems escalated, Boomer was again reenacting his earlier dysfunctional relationships from the orphanage days. Boomer found himself receiving increasingly negative treatment from foster family members: the foster mother was withdrawn (and abandoning), the foster father came close to physically abusing him, and the children were enticed into sexual play with him. Additionally, Boomer was stealing food nightly — though it was plentiful in the house — and he was provoking children at school to beat him up. The reenactment of some of his earliest experiences seemed complete and included — for the grand finale — the wholesale rejection by each foster family in turn.

As in the case of Boomer, the short-term effect of the foster child's reenactment is the eliciting of negative, rejecting responses from foster family members (counter-transference reaction). This is the foster family's often unwitting response to reenactment. (This reaction or response fits into the destructive cycle seen in Table 3.2 above.) Sometimes, despite its resolve to help the child, the foster family finds itself feeling rageful, discouraged, and withdrawn from him. They find their attempts at connecting with the child rebuffed or undermined at every turn.

As for the long term effect, without intervention from a knowledgeable mental health worker and caseworkers, the foster parents' reactions may ultimately result in a termination of the placement, as in the case of Jason below.

*   *   *   *   *

A psychological evaluation of Jason was conducted after his fourth foster placement failure. He was surprisingly unbothered. "She (the foster mother) just didn't like my bad mouth," was his first remark. Only ten-years-old, Jason could swear like a dock worker, but that was the least of his problems. The latest in a parade of placement failures stemmed from the divisive influence he had on marriages. Pure and simple, Jason was a home-wrecker. In each failed placement he had demonstrated an uncanny ability to ally with the foster father and pit him against his mate. What started as a solid marriage at the onset of foster placement was an unsteady wreck after a few short months with Jason. Under the microscope Jason's alliance with the favored parent, i.e. the foster father, was not real intimacy. In fact, the tie to him was exploitive. The alliance was valuable to Jason only in so far as it could be used to ventilate anger towards the other parent.

*   *   *   *   *

The resistance Jason showed to incorporation into a foster family was extreme, but not uncommon. Such stubborn resistance was directly linked to Jason's negative expectations: about the fleeting nature of intimate relationships, about mothers as inevitably rejecting, and about fathers as pawns in the struggle against mothers. In Jason's case this was not merely the initial balking of a child placed with a strange foster home. Jason's behavior functioned to actively sabotage the placement. This boy, having been neglected, abused and ultimately abandoned by his biological mother early in life, later suffered through foster care drift (eight homes in two years). Unfortunately, Jason learned along the way that he had some perverse control in his chaotic world, a world in which he felt utterly impotent. Indeed, Jason could control how close he would let others become and how long he would allow a placement to last. When intimacy demands in his first foster home became too burdensome, Jason told his teacher that his foster father had physically abused him. In a second foster home, Jason again spread lies about the family at school. He told the teacher that the foster mother refused to feed him and that she had attempted to sexually abuse him. In the fourth foster placement attempt, Jason befriended and beguiled the foster father, while he harassed the foster mother when left alone with her. Jason made lewd remarks to her and stole her lingerie, which he shredded.

Again, as with Boomer, Jason's conduct problems, when taken as a whole, culminated in a reenactment of traumatic, abusive, neglecting, and rejecting scenes from his earliest years. Although Jason was mostly unaware of the earliest injuries, physical and psychological, his unconscious negative expectations drove him to certain conduct problems and to the reenactment of his painful past.

Concluding Remarks.

Reenactment in attachment-disordered foster children is typically based upon the view of parent figures as abusive, neglectful, undependable, ungiving, unresponsive and unreliable. Understandable as these perceptions might be, given the horrendous histories of these children, they interfere with change, growth, and healthy attachment formation. Moreover, these perceptions sustain the child's old patterns of interacting (or not interacting) with others.

The negative expectations, conduct problems, and reenactments of the maltreated foster child are the vestiges of harder times in the child's life. Typically, they trigger feelings, reactions, and responses in the foster parents which may jeopardize the stability of the placement, as we will see in the next chapter.

4 | The Foster Parent Response

Foster parents often have a superior grasp of behavior modification techniques, disciplinary skills, and parenting common sense. However, they are often hampered by their own negative reactions to the disturbed foster child's conduct problems and reenactment. In effect they have become victims of the child's negative working model. In Chapter Four discussion turns to foster parent reactions to the child's reenactment of earlier, dysfunctional relationships. Special emphasis will be placed on the most common, intense, emotional reactions which foster parents experience when attempting to raise and help the attachment-disordered child.

Foster Parent Reaction or Counter-transference	•Feelings of Impotence •Urge to Reject the Child •Abusive Impulses towards the Child •Emotional Withdrawal and Depression •Feeling like the Bad Parent •Sexual Feelings for the Child	Table 4.1

Foster Parent Reactions.

Though they might not be immediately aware of the realities of reenactment, foster parents frequently report a variety of intensely bewildering and foreign reactions after the placement of the attachment-disordered child. Psychoanalytically speaking, these reactions might be called countertransference (see Dollard and Miller, 1951). Table 4.1 summarizes some of the common foster parent reactions to placement of the significantly disturbed foster child.

Often foster parents feel unsettling levels of rage, depression, frustration, anxiety, ambivalence, confusion, inadequacy, sexual attraction, revulsion, and/or withdrawal. They often wonder if they are going crazy, or if they might abuse the child. Oftentimes, dormant, unresolved issues from their own past are reawakened by the presence of the disturbed child in their midst.

Frequently, foster parents of attachment-disordered children report that the child will not allow them to reach him. Accordingly, they feel ineffective, unneeded, and perhaps somewhat useless. Some of the most caring, motivated foster parents confess to confusing, alarming feelings they have never felt before towards children, about parenting, and about themselves and their mate. Many feel discouraged about the attachment-disordered child's stubborn refusal to allow intimacy to form.

Foster parents also point to the constant negative behaviors (including conduct problems) which force them into the thankless role of unrelenting disciplinarian. They described the child's reflexive lying over inconsequential matters, which generates feelings of mistrust towards him. In time, these foster parents feel disillusioned, perplexed, and somewhat paralyzed emotionally — impotent to nurture, guide, engage with, and draw close to the child. At some level they find themselves responding in uncharacteristic and perhaps even frightening ways. One foster mother put it this way, "I never felt that I could give this child what he needed. He would not let me be me...to care for him or to give him something. As a matter of fact, I felt that he wanted me to be mean to him, to abuse him even. It was like he wouldn't feel right until I would physically punish him. His main goal seemed to be to get me to reject him and to throw him out of our family...I felt I was slowly changing into some sort of monster with him. I was so frustrated, and he seemed to want it that way. It seemed out of control...I was out of control of myself."

When placed in an awkward, unwanted, undeserved role by the child, the foster parent inevitably will experience any of a number of emotional responses. The emotional responses are more often negative than positive; they may be faint and almost indetectable at first; and they may be poorly identified. However, over time these responses may have a destructive influence on the foster parent's behavior towards the child, towards her mate, towards her biological children. Eventually the negative feelings, which may have remained subconscious and poorly understood, may flood the individual, dominating his/her thoughts. Even experienced foster parents may be appalled, somewhat disoriented, and mortified by the depth of their negative reactions to the child. Without an understanding of these reactions and some tools to handle them, a foster parent might give the child up hastily, i.e. have the child removed from the home. Another foster parent, again without some sense of control and understanding, might emotionally withdraw from the child, thus ending any chance for attachments to form. A third foster parent, confused and hurt by the child's behavior, might become emotionally or physically abusive to the child.

To reduce the destructive impact of reenactment and foster parent response to it, it is important that foster parents (and the caseworkers and mental health workers who assist them) first identify what some of the typical reactions might be. Early recognition of budding reactions allows time to gain understanding and to establish counter measures.

Common reactions include the following: abusive impulses, urge to reject, guilt and self-doubt, disquieting sexual feelings, emotional exhaustion, emotional insulation, good parent-bad parent split, and depression. (Note: This chapter on foster parents and their reactions to reenactment is probably equally relevant to parental responses in adoptive homes. In addition, psychotherapists, caseworkers, and teachers — in dealing with the attachment-disordered child — may experience similar reactions, though perhaps to a lesser degree of intensity.) We will address herein three of the most frequently reported reactions: abusive impulses, the good parent-bad parent split, and the urge to reject.

Abusive Impulses.

Foster parents are often totally perplexed by the feelings of violent anger evoked in them by children with attachment disorders. With some such children, however, it is a most predictable reaction. Many attachment-disordered children, fearful of expressing anger directly themselves, provoke others to anger. As mentioned earlier, foster children often poorly identify and negotiate their own wants, needs, and feelings. Rather than dealing verbally with the frustration and anger arising interpersonally (especially with caretakers), they resort to behavioral expression. As seen in the Appendix, many of the symptoms or conduct problems of the attachment-disordered child are non-verbal expressions of underlying frustration. Many of the behaviors would also qualify as "passive-aggressive." That is, they ventilate anger for the child in oblique fashion. Often times, passive-aggressive behavior is directed towards the foster parent, who reacts predictably with anger. It is as if the foster parent expresses the anger which the disturbed child finds to be inutterable. The depth and frequency of these angry feelings appall foster parents, many of whom may have been drawn to this work by a desire to express love, affection, and concern for less fortunate, dependent individuals. The strength of their rage is frightening to many foster parents, unfamiliar with such strong negative feelings in themselves. These feelings range from constant exasperation with the child to the growing urge to abuse the child. While foster parents are often loathe to report these feelings, such sentiments are typical in work with attachment-disordered children, as seen below.

* * * * *

Mrs. R., a treatment foster mother with her first attachment-disordered child, looked drawn and haggard. She made poor eye contact and spoke in a voice which cracked with emotion. Her caseworker had sent her to me because the foster placement of little Bobby was in deep jeopardy. Although she was unable to voice her true feelings for several sessions, finally Mrs. R. admitted to violent nightmares about Bobby. She seemed deeply distressed about having murderous dreams at night, and she feared loss of control of her temper during the day. The intensity of the anger was foreign to her.

Mrs. R. had never felt such rage towards her two young biological children, nor towards previous foster children (who had been physically or mentally handicapped but not attachment-disordered). She stated that her husband, a very rational, calm man, lacked similar feelings and thus poorly understood her strong reactions. In my later private conversation with Mr. R., he revealed his fear that his wife was beginning to lose her mind.

*   *   *   *   *

Attachment-disordered children are often masterful at denying anger, while making foster parents' lives miserable. As mentioned above, these maltreated children evoke anger in the foster parent through passive-aggressive behavior. For example, Bobby, in the case presented above, would conveniently "forget" things which brought out the anger in his foster mother, who was an organized, orderly woman. This boy, for instance, left the water running in the bathtub until it overflowed onto the floor and flooded the basement. Bobby next left the backyard gate open, though he was repeatedly reminded that the younger children might run out into traffic. When asked to help in the kitchen, Bobby sneakily threw glasses and silverware away in the trash rather than putting them in the dishwasher. When confronted about his "forgetfulness," he merely shrugged, refused eye contact, and muttered, "I forgot."

As could be expected, many attachment-disordered children come from physically abusive families. It has long been known that abused children often elicit angry, abusive treatment from new caretakers. In fact, many foster parents report that the child seems to seek physical discipline out of habit. Since many maltreated children have been "conditioned" to avoid expression of any feelings or needs directly, they express them in convoluted, indirect, clandestine, and maladaptive ways. These maladaptive expressions by the foster child often elicit the strong reactions from foster parents which we address here. These maladaptive expressions also appear to secure negative attention, to undermine intimacy and to de-stabilize the placement. As we will see in the next chapter, successful treatment of attachment-disordered children rests on teaching them the identification, expression, and negotiation of feelings, and conflicts and needs.)

Mrs. R.'s feelings of homicidal rage, as might be expected, were very disturbing to her. A very kind, gentle woman by nature, she had never experienced anything like this before. In previous work with handicapped and mentally retarded foster children, Mrs. R. had been a very poised, competent mother-figure. Imagine her surprise — and that of her husband and caseworker

— when she voiced abusive, murderous fantasies concerning Bobby. Only after her reactions were placed under her control and when she and her husband were equipped with techniques to confront the child's reenactment, did the murderous fantasies subside. (It should be mentioned here that it is easy to view foster (and adoptive) parents mistakenly as the source of the child's problems, given the disturbing nature of the reactions they report. What can easily be forgotten by professionals is the fact that the foster parent has imported psychopathology into the home. The strongly negative foster parent response which follows is often a reaction to this psychopathology, not the cause of it.)

As in the case of Mr. and Mrs. R. and Bobby, successful intervention often includes the following: didactic information on conduct problems, reenactment, and usual foster parent reactions; support from other experienced therapeutic foster parents; psychotherapy with the child and family; and, the identification and resolution of negative working models, conduct problems, reenactment, and foster parents' reactions, as we see below. (In Chapter Five focus will shift to interventions to be used with reenactment and the foster child's negative working model. But first we will address the working through of foster parents' negative reactions.)

* * * * *

Mrs. R. seemed notably relieved after the "confession" of her homicidal fantasies, especially when she was informed that her reaction was both common and "normal," given the circumstances. Her thoughts about herself as a monster subsided very quickly when she participated in a foster parent support group, wherein more experienced treatment foster parents spoke openly of similar feelings. Hearing other foster parents express "taboo" feelings gave her permission to more openly discuss her own pent-up hostilities towards Bobby. Soon, Mrs. R. could even speak somewhat jokingly about those fantasies. She seemed less brittle, guilt-ridden, and self-doubting. As she grew more comfortable with her feelings, she felt less controlled by the anger. Also, as she could understand and accept her own deep feelings, she became much more effective in helping Bobby express his repressed emotion.

In individual consultation sessions with me, Mrs. R. spoke of her own repressive family background, which had poorly prepared her for the likes of Bobby. Raised in a family which was close-knit but non-verbal, Mrs. R. had never witnessed open confrontation, and never recalled any deeply felt anger towards her parents, even during her adolescence. Mrs. R. was a woman who desired closeness and felt little anger. For his part, Bobby was a child who feared yet seethed with anger. Not surprisingly, Mrs. R.'s successful, tender-loving-care approach with handicapped foster children was doomed to fail with Bobby. (Bobby reenacted his own early history with Mrs. R., much to her chagrin. A boy who had been sorely neglected and repeatedly abused, Bobby perceived parent figures as fearsome and ungiving. A secretly angry boy, Bobby had learned to express his frustration/rage indirectly towards the dangerous adults around him. Indeed, he may have derived some satisfaction in evoking anger in parents. In this situation, Mrs. R.'s uncharacteristic anger was directly related to Bobby's reenactment.) After living with and relating to Bobby for some time, she had in common with Bobby's abusive parents an almost constant urge to hurt him.

In the consultation sessions, Mrs. R. was encouraged to verbalize her frightening anger towards Bobby. She was repeatedly shown how the anger derived from: (1) Bobby's passive-aggressive, provocative behavior towards her and (2) from a frustration of her strong desire to give to and receive love from this child. With increasing insight, Mrs. R. seemed less controlled by Bobby's machinations. She was able to adopt a more "clinical," dispassionate perspective towards Bobby, which reduced to a more modest level her need to give and receive. This rendered her less vulnerable to Bobby's rejection of her offers; correspondingly, it made her less threatening to Bobby, who had become phobic of the requirements of intimacy.

During psychotherapy sessions with Bobby, Mr. and Mrs. R. were encouraged to be present. The approach used was highly confrontive, because Bobby was so very passive, oppositional, avoidant, deceitful, and shallow. Bobby wore an almost constant grin on his face and spoke in lilting voice, as he maintained that he was perfectly content in the foster home. He adamantly — but oh, so politely — denied any anger towards the foster parents or their biological children. Initially, Bobby refused to express any feelings of mistrust, rage, jealousy, disappointment, hurt, or even difference of opinion. However, some gains were made by pressing Bobby on how he truly felt about: being placed in foster care; rivalrous feelings towards the biological children; anger at being punished for his misbehavior; the foster parents taking "respite week-ends" by themselves; and visits which his biological parents cut short or missed altogether.

The foster parents, during these sessions, were told that Bobby needed more than "TLC." They were told that no corrective attachment could form, and that their own unsettling rage would continue, unless we elicited underlying feelings from Bobby. Telling them about it — and then showing them how it could be done — gave Mr. and Mrs. R. permission to attempt confrontation in the sessions and at home. Soon, they were as effective at confrontation as the therapist. At home, following a most successful confrontation session, Bobby finally dropped his smile completely, then angrily spewed forth a great number of rage-filled comments about how the foster family hated him, how he hated them, and how they treated him unfairly and loved him less than their own children. These uncensored statements tumbled out for several uninterrupted minutes, until the tears came. Bobby's anger evolved into a profound sadness; he was racked with sobs as the foster mother held him close. Interestingly, she reported that Bobby for the first time allowed her to hold him at her initiation. She remarked that he seemed to sink into her with a feeling of surrender.

As one might expect, treatment of Bobby did not end after one sincere, poignant moment. Bobby, after a day or two of relative calm and closeness, reverted to his old self, to his comfortable reenactment. The foster parents were encouraged to continue "truth telling" sessions with Bobby as often as needed. Both parents, though not confrontive by nature, showed tremendous ability to learn. Ultimately, after months of confrontation, Bobby appeared to speak more candidly about his feelings, and to relate more genuinely and closely to Mr. and Mrs. R. His tendency to reenact diminished and he seemed to permit the beginning of honest, intimate relating. (Unfortunately, in this case, Bobby was returned to his birth parents, though they had refused any help for themselves. Within months Bobby was removed again and placed in residential treatment, as his behavior had escalated to a dangerous degree.) Bobby's temporary improvement in foster placement was at least in part due to growth in the foster parents — to their increased understanding of their emotional response to Bobby's negative expectations and attempts to reenact.

The Good Parent/Bad Parent Split.

Commonly, foster mothers and fathers end up feeling quite differently about the foster child, about themselves as parents, and about their spouses as parents. It is not uncommon for the foster father, for example, to feel like a good parent, while his wife feels like a bad parent. As mentioned above, in the case of Bobby, Mr. R. wondered if his wife's homicidal fantasies indicated a loss of mental balance.

Commonly, the father figure perceives the placed child much differently than the mother. There is a good reason for this, one found in how attachment-disordered children reenact in the foster (or adoptive) home. Typically, foster children have accumulated greater feelings of resentment towards mother-figures. Yet, they have more often been raised by mothers, and thus have a tendency to gravitate towards them. Accordingly, disturbed foster children have highly potent, unresolved feelings of anxiety, ambivalence, and anger towards the mother-figure, their primary caretaker. There are some good reasons for such potency of feeling towards the mother. The attachment-disordered child may have been emotionally or physically abandoned by the mother and/or may have grown attached to and later lost several mother-figures.

Meanwhile, father figures often have been absent or peripheral to the process of attachment/separation/loss. They have not been primary attachment figures in many cases, and their loss may be experienced as less traumatic and less infuriating to the child. Oftentimes, father figures, when involved, have been more intimidating, abusive figures. Any anger felt towards them may have been suppressed and directed towards the mother. Consequently, these fathers bequeath to later father figures (foster or adoptive) somewhat fewer problems with the foster child. (Admittedly, there are exceptions here. Some foster fathers are in very troubling circumstances with these children. For example, these fathers may find themselves shunned and avoided by foster children, who have been abused or neglected by their earlier male caretakers. Additionally, when the attachment-disordered foster child has been sexually abused by a past male caretaker, she may bring to the relationship with the foster father seductive, coy behavior which puts him off or confuses him.) Foster fathers are usually less involved in the day to day caretaking of the placed child, and they often develop a more playful, less intense, less disciplinary relationship to the child. More involved in the nitty-gritty interactions and discipline with the foster child, foster mothers become much more easily embroiled in the child's reenactment, as seen below.

* * * * *

Alan, a taxing, defiant seven-year-old foster child, was available for adoption legally, though he was anything but adoptable. His current foster mother, Mrs. O., was the target of a great deal of anger, as Alan perpetually engaged her in power struggles when Mr. O. was not at home. However, as soon as Mr. O. came home from work, Alan transformed into a smiling, cooperative boy who presented no observable problems to anyone. When Mrs. O. recounted her day with her husband, he could not believe that she was talking about the same child. In an attempt to help his wife, Mr. O. offered advice about how to handle Alan better. Mrs. O. felt misunderstood and patronized, while Mr. O. assumed that his wife was exaggerating her concerns or, worse yet, that she was the cause of Alan's problem. Marital problems ensued.

* * * * *

In this case, consultation from the mental health worker entailed much more than sharing of didactic information about attachment problems. Mr. O. was told repeatedly about Alan's tendency to direct his anger at the "bad parent," i.e. the mother figure, while sparing the "good parent," the father. However, theoretical information sharing was not enough to convince Mr. O. at a deeper level. Without correcting Mr. O.'s perception of Alan and without changing his role with Alan, no improvement could be made. Accordingly, the mental health worker devised a plan to assist the family. Mrs. O. was removed from her role as disciplinarian. The couple drew up a mutually agreed upon list of behaviors which would be punishable. And Mr. O. was given the role of exclusive disciplinarian. In a matter of two weeks, Mr. O. came to observe Alan the way his wife had. Alan began stealing things from Mr. O.'s workshop, and then he lied when confronted with the evidence. Mr. O. also found himself in power struggles with Alan on a daily (and nightly basis). For her part, Mrs. O. appeared more relaxed and actually found Alan reaching out to her more positively. (This reaching out, however, did not indicate true attachment formation at this juncture.)

At this point in the intervention, Alan's negative working model was undoubtedly unchanged. Though his conduct problems, and resultant reenactment had changed in focus from Mrs. O. to Mr. O., the underlying perception of caretakers would still be negative, and for the most part, unconscious and unverbalized. While the shift in roles between foster parents gave Mrs. O. some relief, the intervention had to proceed further, as seen next.

* * * * *

Once Mr. O. had achieved some "experiential insight" with Alan, he was primed for cooperating with Mrs. O. in some interventions designed to limit and confront Alan's acting-out, while promoting honest emotional expression from the boy and ultimately the beginning of healthier attachments. As with Mr. and Mrs. T. and Bobby above, Mr. and Mrs. O. were helped to engage in effective confrontations of Alan's manipulation, deceit, shallowness, and passive-resistance. Alan, in a number of stormy family therapy sessions, was pushed to the point of expressing his true views about women/mothers, who he described, colorfully, as "a bunch of whores who leave you and don't really care about what happens to you." With true conviction he bet Mr. O. that Mrs. O. would probably leave him too, because women were "all that way." However, he staunchly denied any sadness about losing his birth mother and his third foster mother — who had kept him for over two years before her tragic death.

Mr. O., who had become quite expert at confrontation, challenged Alan's denial with some very fitting remarks. He commented, "I don't believe that you have no feelings for Mrs. M. (the third foster mother). Your books, your papers, your toys are all torn up, but you keep her pictures safe. You even screamed at Tommy (a younger birth child), when he went near your photo album. It's the only thing you take care of." Of course, Alan denied this, but after Mr. O. repeated the simple phrase, "You love her pictures; yes, you do," like a broken record for a few minutes, Alan angrily blurted out that the foster father should "shut up" about Mrs. M.; that he had no right to talk about her; that it was none of his business how he felt. Confrontation went on for several more minutes, with Mr. O.'s relentless barrage, softened somewhat by Mrs. O.'s intermittent statements to Alan that it was okay to talk about how much he loved Mrs. M. Eventually, Alan erupted with unbridled hostility, letting out a torrent of tearful anger which melted into deep sobs. Although he did not let Mrs. O. touch and hold him for perhaps forty-five minutes, he ultimately let down his guard, after he was emotionally spent. She caressed him while he seemed to meld into her gradually. He cried on for another thirty minutes, answering that he had loved Mrs. M—still did—and wanted to be with her again.

* * * * *

As you might expect, it is rare that one, solitary "breakthrough" moment in therapy is enough to solder lasting changes in children with significant attachment problems. What is more likely is that moments such as the one above must be repeated in therapy sessions and in the foster home. It is the job of the mental health worker to help the foster parents understand the need for extraordinary parenting interventions such as the one described above. Indeed, it is in the foster home where many emotionally loaded situations offer themselves as grist for the treatment mill. Foster parents need to be trained and prepared for those situations when they arise; emotionally charged encounters should not be reserved for the psychotherapy hour. In the child's living environment, the foster parents are in a key position to intervene therapeutically with the attachment-disordered child.

Of interest in this case is the fact that Alan eventually grew quite close and attached to both Mr. and Mrs. O. It appeared that the repeated verbalizing of the previously unstated, unconscious negative working model opened up possibilities for honest communication. Alan's admission of his strongly felt anger about past (and present) losses reduced the need to communicate non-verbally through conduct problems. In turn, the reduction in conduct problems decreased reenactment and negative foster parent response to Alan. These barriers aside, attachments were more likely to take place and, in fact, did form, as Alan remained in long-term foster placement with the O. family.

Urge to Reject.

Another common foster parent reaction to reenactment is that of the urge to reject the child. When the unattached child senses a growing intimacy in the foster family, he anticipates the rejection he has historically experienced throughout his life. That is, his negative working model prepares him for abandonment, rejection, abuse and non-acceptance. (He feels about himself that he is worthless/unwanted, unsafe, and impotent.) He often, then, based upon his negative expectations, reenacts the familiar drama of rejection. Specifically, he behaves in such a way (though not always consciously) to bring on the expected rejection. (This may give the foster child some sense of safety and control in frighteningly intimate situations.) In response, the foster parents often react with the urge to reject, as we see in the next case.

* * * * *

Laura, age five, had been in twelve foster homes in the previous three years. Deemed unadoptable due to the behavior problems which had wrecked previous placements, Laura was placed in therapeutic foster care. Soon thereafter, the foster parents reported that a clear pattern emerged. Each time they felt that Laura was growing closer to them, improving behaviorally or accomplishing things for which she was praised, the foster parents would observe a sharp deterioration in good behavior. More precisely, Laura was expert at making herself repulsive, at times when she was becoming most attractive to the foster parents. For example, when she sat on the foster parents' lap, she instantly had a "gas attack." When she was put to bed, she began picking at old sores until they bled. On a daily basis, she started soiling her underwear, which she hid in her drawer of clean clothes. On one occasion, after the foster mother praised her artwork from preschool, Laura flushed the papers down the toilet, clogging the plumbing. (And she refused to draw anymore in preschool.) It appeared that Laura was, by her every act, undermining progress and begging for rejection.

* * * * *

While many foster children actively sabotage closeness — as in the case of Laura — others are simply withdrawn, passive, and unresponsive to the foster parents. Often they lack the desire, ability or energy to interact with others in a mutually rewarding way. "Emotional blobs," their lack of interpersonal hunger ultimately discourages others from engaging them.

It is worth underscoring here that many foster parents initially appear (to the mental health worker) to be indifferent and cool in relationship to their attachment-disordered foster child. These foster parents have become cloaked in emotional insulation. After having experienced repeated failure with their attachment-disordered foster child, they withdraw self-protectively.

It is easy to misidentify these foster parents as the essence of the child's problem, as the cause of his increasingly difficult, outlandish behaviors or of his passive withdrawal from the family. However, oftentimes the emotional insulation we observe in the foster parents is the result not the cause of the child's abnormal behavior. More specifically, the emotional insulation seen in foster parents is a clue to the child's on-going reenactment and to his underlying negative working model. Importantly, emotional insulation and the urge to reject, if left unattended, can hasten the demise of a placement, as in the case of Laurelei below.

* * * * *

Laurelei was a pretty, but emotionally empty seven-year-old girl who gave nothing back to her foster parents. Laurelei was not yet free for adoption, though her birth mother had abandoned her months before and had never appeared for any court proceedings. Laurelei was quite apathetic overall. Her smile was manufactured. Her eyes stared vacantly, as she bared her teeth in a wooden grin. Although not mentally retarded, she seemed oddly dim-witted, rarely providing foster parents with any feedback that she understood what they told her. At bedtime, she doled out limp hugs. When she talked, she rarely showed any child-like enthusiasm, rather, droning on without inflection. If she answered a question, she never elaborated, mostly answering with, "I don't know," or "Maybe."

Laurelei never verbalized anger to the foster parents, although she would often hurt the younger children in the home and would argue with them and verbally abuse them — out of earshot of the foster parents. After months of caring for this child, the foster parents felt apologetic about their request to have her moved. "She has never really been a behavior problem at all...we can't really put our finger on it...she's not really a bad girl, in any major way...in fact, she is at times almost unrealistically good." It appeared that these foster parents suffered from the "cumulative effect of inertia" — the insidious depletion of emotional energy which appears in a relationship with a child who is "dead" inside.

*   *   *   *   *

In the case of Laurelei, the placement was salvaged, although in many such instances irreparable damage is done before mental health intervention can begin. Fortunately, Laurelei's foster parents were stalwart and had good support systems in place. Laurelei was placed briefly in respite care, at the suggestion of the mental health worker. Respite care enabled the foster parents to recuperate, to re-examine their committment to this unfulfilling child, and to strategize the course of intervention with the therapist, as we see below.

*   *   *   *   *

After reviewing the situation with the caseworker and foster parents and evaluating Laurelei, the therapist concluded that she showed the vestiges of a neglectful, unstimulating, emotionally impoverished upbringing. She was a silently angry child who typically suppressed anger towards the adult world. Although not consciously attempting to spoil her foster placement, Laurelei's unresponsiveness had discouraged and distanced the foster parents. In essence, Laurelei had a thoroughly negative working model regarding caretakers and herself, and she was reenacting the familiar course of rejection.

The therapist asked the foster parents to overlook Laurelei's indifference and to give her what she needed — but would not ask for on her own. Daily "holding and hugging" was prescribed by the therapist. The foster mother and father took turns in placing Laurelei on their laps and holding and rocking her for twenty minutes, three times per day. The parents were told to hold her tightly, bounce her, tickle her playfully, and otherwise stimulate her. They were asked, essentially, to enliven this child. Laurelei routinely offered nominal resistance to the holding sessions, but seemed to enjoy the interchanges after they had begun in earnest.

During the sessions, the child made better eye contact. Her face brightened and eyes sparkled. The foster father was encouraged to wrestle and roughhouse with Laurelei, who seemed completely unused to this at first. After a relatively gentle start, the foster father stated that Laurelei began to actually fight back with more forcefulness. He reported, much to his surprise, that Laurelei soon began to laugh during the wrestling matches. Beyond that, she even began to initiate wrestling at times during the day other than the scheduled sessions.

As Laurelei became more spontaneous physically, she was then helped to vocalize some true emotion. It was assumed by the therapist, that Laurelei had bottled up a great deal of anger. A number of approaches were attempted to elicit some expression of unspoken anger. The foster parents reported some increasing success in the use of "mock arguments" with Laurelei. The foster parents were encouraged to continue and to increase these "pretend fights." In particular, the foster mother seemed quite skilled at staging mock arguments with Laurelei. For example, she would tease Laurelei about her hair being blond, when it was actually black. Next, she might tell Laurelei to do something ridiculous, such as to carry the refrigerator out to the garage. Laurelei, in the face of the silly, impossible request, would protest. The foster mother would take the ridiculous to the absurd by pressing the request further and further.

Although such mock arguments were truly ludicrous, they allowed Laurelei the opportunity to disagree, even if in fun. Correspondingly, in therapy sessions, the therapist attempted to provoke emotional reactions in Laurelei. A combination of humor, teasing, confrontation, and modeling were employed to elicit more animated, spontaneous, forceful responses from Laurelei. After several weeks of intervention, the foster parents reported that Laurelei would unilaterally approach them for hugs, that she had begun to write them love notes, and that she had begun to disagree with them in the home over issues of importance to her. The foster mother stated, "I feel that she is starting to respond to me. I feel less like I have no impact on her. I think he is behaving like a real child with some emotion for once."

* * * * *

Not all disturbed children respond to mock arguments and forced lap time with the foster parents. Indeed, Laurelei was only mildly attachment-disordered and showed less resistance than many disturbed children. Mental health intervention, nonetheless, was instrumental in breaking a cycle (of reenactment and foster parent reaction) that would likely have ended in a terminated placement. As importantly, it allowed for the beginning of a relationship between the child and the foster parents which permitted some attachment formation. As is often the case, the foster parent involvement or re-involvement was central to the child's improvement. Laurelei's reenactment of abandonment and rejection had stimulated a defeatist attitude on the part of the foster parents who came close to rejecting Laurelei. Mental health involvement promoted the re-involvement by the foster parents who then refused the child's rejection. There is nothing more destructive to the successful foster home placement than the foster parents' growing sense of futility and powerlessness. With the child who stubbornly reenacts, foster parents often feel increasing levels of impotence and uselessness. They do not experience any parental sense of satisfaction and worth, any sense that their involvement with the child is accomplishing anything. Essentially, they come to feel like failures as parents, and, in due course recoil from and/or reject the child.) It is the primary role of the mental health worker (and other professionals involved in the case) to support the foster parents in their therapeutic role with their foster child.

A Word of Caution to Helping Professionals.

It is a sad fact that foster parents frequently have found themselves ignored, overlooked, and excluded from the treatment process. Even though they might be the single most effective treatment agents with attachment-disordered children, foster parents have unfortunately been relegated to the lowest rung on the treatment ladder. In regards to the child's psychotherapy, some foster parents have even been barred from participation in the sessions.

This unfortunate exclusion of foster parents may be based upon the false assumption that the psychotherapist holds the key to change in seriously disturbed foster children. That assumption may justify omitting the truly central figures in the overall treatment of the disturbed child, i.e. the foster parents. Indeed, without carefully and continually involving foster parents in the treatment process, the mental health professional may actually do more harm than good — for example, by interfering with the tenuous relationship between the child and the foster parents. If the psychotherapist develops a "close relationship" with an attachment-disordered child — a child with tremendous fear of family intimacy — the child may have an escape route — a less threatening alternative to attaching to foster parents. (It is a less threatening alternative because the foster child may easily develop a "pseudo-attachment," one marked by idealization of the therapist as "perfect parent." Often, the attachment-disordered child prefers pseudo-attachments to neighbors, school personnel, psychotherapists, caseworkers, and perfect strangers. These pseudo-attachments can prevent the development of genuine attachments within the foster placement.) In sum, by permitting and/or inviting the child to attach to him, the therapist might unwittingly interfere with or delay the process of attachment formation in the foster home.

Failure to involve the foster parents in treatment in an active way can also result in treatment efforts running at cross purposes. For instance, the psychotherapist may conduct his sessions, relatively oblivious to how the child's is doing "in the real world," as seen next.

* * * * *

One very experienced and talented foster mother labelled it, "Taxi Cab Psychotherapy." She would drive up to the therapist's office and drop the child off at the door. The therapist never asked her in, past the introductory session. The therapist never knew that the child had set a fire in the garage next door. He never knew about the chronic stealing that the child did from the pantry. The foster mother was limited to the role of transportation, she was only the "cab driver" for her foster son, a seriously attachment-disordered youngster. This woman could only guess whether psychotherapy was going in the right direction. The psychologist never conferred with her about coordinating psychotherapy with treatment efforts in the home. Unfortunately, the therapist was ignorant of the growing exhaustion in the home, which ultimately resulted in the child being moved.

* * * * *

In the case presented above, the foster parents had a strongly negative reaction to their foster son, who was reenacting his characteristic abandonment/rejection drama. Sadly, the psychotherapist was unaware that the placement was in dire straits. By the time he found out about it, it was too late to save the placement.

This mental health professional, using an exclusionary approach to psychotherapy, established what he felt was a "strong bond" with the foster child. However, he failed to concentrate on supporting the foster family; on helping them to understand the child's negative expectations, conduct problems, and penchant for reenactment; on assisting them in understanding and gaining control over their negative reactions to the child; on working with them to stabilize placement; and on fostering attachments between themselves and their foster child.

Exclusion of the foster parent from the treatment process also can present another danger — namely, that the therapist can become allied too closely with the disturbed child and his misperceptions (influenced by his negative working model) of the foster family. Overidentified with the foster child in individual psychotherapy sessions, even skilled mental health workers may fall prey to the child who "opens up" with complaints about alleged mistreatment in the foster home. Unknowingly duped by this one-sided information, the psychotherapist seizes upon these complaints as the source of the child's current difficulties. Meanwhile, the therapist develops a "warm and trusting" relationship to the child, who acts quite differently in the therapy hour than in the foster home. The therapist, truly seeing a different child than the foster parents, trusts his perceptions while doubting theirs. Rather than supporting and collaborating with the foster parents, the therapist then becomes a misguided advocate for the child and a judgmental adversary of the foster parent. In the all-too-frequent "worst case" scenario, the child becomes totally unmanageable in the foster home, and the foster parents, incriminated and unsupported, ask for the child to be removed. To reduce the chances for such a sad outcome, the therapist must aggressively involve the foster parents in treatment of the child. At a minimum the therapist should meet with the foster parents before and after each session with the child. (In some cases it may be appropriate to include the foster parents for entire therapy sessions.) The therapist, armed with information on the child's progress or backsliding during the week, can raise issues with the child which otherwise might be lost. The following case study shows how the therapist can miss the mark therapeutically when the foster parents are uninvolved in treatment of the child.

* * * * *

Bobby easily befriended the therapist, who mistakenly thought she was befriending Bobby. Bobby, at ten years of age, had already seen more "therapist-types" than this therapist had seen attachment-disordered foster children. Quickly, Bobby began to ally with the therapist by, at first "reluctantly," and later more and more willingly disclosing how emotionally stingy the foster mother was. An excerpt from the session shows how Bobby proceeded:

Bobby: "Yes, she never has any time for me at all. She is always too busy with everybody else in the house...I come in last place."

Therapist: "That must be frustrating, Bobby. But you have to understand

that she has other children in the house to attend to."
  Bobby: "I know. But I never get any time with her alone."
  Therapist: "Foster care is not an easy place to be, is it?"

* * * * *

What the therapist did not know was that Bobby always set himself up for rejection. He inevitably asked for attention when the foster mother was tied up with someone else. For example, if someone were injured or crying, Bobby would demand her focus when she was busy bandaging or cuddling. On the other side, whenever the foster mother attempted to give Bobby positive attention, he rebuffed her. Bobby, whose history showed him to be sorely neglected, compulsively reenacted that history within the foster home.

Concluding Remarks.

As seen above, the foster child's conduct problems and reenactment can trigger intensely bewildering, negative responses and reactions in the foster parents. These reactions can spell trouble for placement, if they are not understood and resolved.

After living for weeks or months with the attachment-disordered child, foster parents often find themselves ensnared in endless negative interactions with the child. The urge to abuse, reject, or withdraw from the child grows strong. In situations like this, the mental health professional can become part of the solution or part of the problem. If he works collaboratively with the foster parents, he may enable them to become highly effective change agents for the disturbed child. However, if his work becomes exclusionary, the mental health professional may unknowingly interfere with the placement.

In the next chapter, we will discuss more specifically how certain non-exclusionary psychotherapeutic approaches can be used to alter the negative working model.

5 Psychotherapy With Attachment-Disordered Children

Foster placement can be ineffective without a change in the foster child's underlying expectations about himself, his caretakers, and the world around him. Psychotherapy can play a part in altering the negative expectations, assumptions, and working model.

Chapter Five outlines four central components to psychotherapeutic intervention with the attachment-disordered foster child. The mental health approaches described herein differ substantially from those used with less disturbed children. A detailed case example will be presented to clarify the use of psychotherapy in altering the negative working model.

An Unorthodox Psychotherapy Approach.

Deeply ingrained negative expectations may not respond — in serious attachment disorder cases — to conventional mental health approaches, such as non-directive play therapy, insight-oriented psychotherapy, and standard family therapy. Indeed, the altering of the resistant negative working model frequently necessitates somewhat unorthodox mental health approaches (Speltz, 1990; Masterson, 1972; Magid and McKelvey, 1987). The decision to employ unorthodox interventions must be based upon a thorough evaluation of the child, his attachment-disorder, and the foster family system. As seen in Table 5.1, psychotherapy with attachment-disordered foster children is composed of four central components, the focus of which is to alter the negative working model. These components are:

1. Containing conduct problems (which comprise the reenactment and which precipitate negative reactions in the foster parents and often neutralize or jeopardize the placement);

2. Increasing verbalization of the underlying negative working model;

3. Fostering communication of the needs and feelings of the attachment-disordered child and the negotiation of differences between the child and the foster parents; and

4. Promoting positive encounters between the foster parents and the child. These encounters would include increased acceptance by the child of nurturance and positive caretaking from the foster parents.

As seen in the preceding chapter, therapeutic efforts by the foster family, sometimes with guidance from the mental health worker, are pivotal in producing change in the child. Indeed, in the best of circumstances the foster parents and mental health professional will collaborate in the use of the four components outlined above. That is, treatment in the home parallels that in the office.

| *Four Components In Altering the Negative Working Model* | 1. **Containing Conduct Problems**
 2. **Increasing Verbalization of the NWM**
 3. **Fostering Communication of Needs and Negotiation of Differences**
 4. **Promoting Positive Encounters** | **Table 5.1** |

Case Study.

To illustrate how psychotherapy contributes to the overall treatment of the attachment-disordered foster child, a case will be presented in some detail.

* * * * *

Barry, a seriously attachment-disordered foster child, had been — by the age of ten — placed in numerous foster homes and had failed in two adoptive placements. (Barry's two younger siblings, who were less disturbed, remained in the home with the birth mother.) After a year-long stay in a residential treatment center, Barry was placed with a therapeutic foster family. Within a short period of time, the foster family reported a long list of conduct problems, which included the following: withdrawal/avoidance, habitual lying, stealing of food, roaming the house at night, fire setting, passive face-to-face compliance with the foster parents, destructiveness to prized possessions of the foster parents, and anger directed at younger children in the home.

The foster parents stated that Barry was very difficult to like, that he seemed insincere, smiling at them in a reflexive way. They stated, additionally, that Barry never showed any direct anger to them, seemed unable/unwilling to ask for his needs to be met, and essentially isolated himself from them emotionally. The foster placement, according to the caseworker, was in jeopardy due to Barry's hurtful, assaultive behavior towards the younger children and due to his night foraging, both of which alarmed the foster parents.

History revealed that Barry, a mulatto boy, had been born to a low-functioning Caucasian woman who had turned to prostitution to fund her heroin addiction. Barry, as an infant, had been horribly neglected and malnourished by his mother, and periodically he had been physically abused by his mother's pimps or boyfriends. (The birth mother's own history was rife with abuse, neglect and sexual victimization by her stepfather and older stepbrothers. Attachments to her family of origin were marginal.)

Although Barry and his mother had been known to the welfare system from the earliest weeks of his life, he was placed in foster care for the first time at the age of three. The birth mother reported that Barry was too demanding, stole food, and made her feel like "beating him to death." Subsequently, Barry went back and forth between foster homes and his mother's home, until the age of five, at which time the mother disappeared forever, apparently taking two younger children with her. Termination proceedings were completed within two years and Barry was freed for adoption. In rapid succession, two adoptive attempts failed due to escalating conduct problems; Barry was placed in foster care and eventually a residential treatment center. Ultimately, he was placed in the Jones therapeutic foster home, where he resided at the time psychotherapy began.

* * * * *

The above case presentation is representative of many maltreated, attachment-disordered children. Barry, as a result of his early history, presented as significantly attachment-disordered with strong insecurity, ambivalence, and resistance. He had become a deeply, but quietly, rageful boy with little or no trust in caretakers. His negative working model contained perceptions of caretakers as undependable, stingy, frightening, and ultimately abandoning. Perceptions of himself were that he was worthless, bad, unsafe, and impotent with adults. The effect of his conduct problems was to both increase caretaking behavior and to reject and punish the caretaker. In the Jones therapeutic foster home, conduct problems (in combination) had already begun to reproduce old relationships with these new caretakers. Indeed, Mr. and Mrs. Jones had begun to respond to the reenactment in a predictably negative fashion. The resultant drama ultimately stemmed from the negative working model of this unfortunate, attachment-disordered foster child.

The four components of psychotherapy, as described above, guided the treatment of Barry and his negative working model. We will attempt next to describe how these components unfolded during psychotherapy/consultation.

1. Containing Conduct Problems.

Containing conduct problems serves two functions: one, to reduce behaviors which endanger the placement and prevent attachment formation; and two, to decrease the indirect, non-verbal ways in which the child expresses his negative working model (in the hope that verbal modes can be explored.)

In the case of Barry above, containment took many forms. The psychotherapist recognized that the assaultive behavior towards the younger children was a sign of displacement. That is, Barry displaced most of his anger onto the safe target of the younger children in the home. As you will recall, Barry never showed direct expression of anger towards the foster parents (indeed, Barry had never displayed openly his anger towards any caretakers). This pattern stemmed from Barry's underlying negative expectations, which characterized caretakers as too ominous and threatening for honest, verbal expressions of anger from him. Barry, therefore, would vent anger towards hapless younger children, while avoiding any and all direct expressions of anger towards the foster parents.

In meetings with the foster parents, the psychotherapist advised them to punish (i.e. through "time-out") Barry each time he acted out towards the other children. Accordingly, Barry was sent to sit on a chair in the corner of the room. He was also "debriefed" by the foster parents after each time out (of usually ten to fifteen minutes). Barry was not allowed out of the corner, until he admitted that he had not liked being placed in the chair by the foster parents. The "not liking" expression was a mild verbalization of his present conflict with the foster parent. It was hoped that the time-out and the subsequent debriefing would curtail Barry's acting-out and, perhaps more importantly, generate immediate, specific feelings of anger towards the foster parents. (Feelings of anger towards the foster parents, of course, were habitually suppressed by Barry.) These immediate, specific feelings of anger, then, would become grist for the therapeutic mill. The focus could be directed away from issues between Barry and the younger children, and onto the underlying, previously unverbalized, issue between Barry and caretakers.

Interestingly, acting-out towards the other children increased temporarily, as Barry became silently angry at the foster parents for punishing him, taking sides, etc. To Barry, his angry expressions towards the children seemed, in his convoluted thinking, justified. His anger at caretakers was increased when the time-out/debriefing procedure was begun. At the same time, Barry's verbalizations of his anger towards the foster parents during debriefing were meager. That is, his beginning attempts at vocalizing anger directly to the foster parents provided insufficient release, especially at the beginning. Thus, he was even angrier at the foster parents and yet was still expressing only a small portion of his anger towards them directly. Predictably, acting-out towards the younger children increased, though only temporarily.

It is important to point out here that, when used alone, behavior modification approaches (e.g. time out procedures) often fail with attachment-disordered children. These approaches are apt to produce some superficial changes in "surface behavior," while underlying negative working models generate new conduct problems. It is only when containment approaches are used jointly with the other treatment components that deeper, lasting changes appear.

2. Increasing Verbalization.

As mentioned above, containing conduct problems is insufficient, on its own, to reduce reenactment and to produce meaningful change in the child's attachment disorder. Indeed, it is essential to alter the underlying negative working model to which the attachment-disordered child adheres. One way in which that is accomplished is to elicit statements, thoughts, and feelings from the child about himself, his caretakers, and life in general. Containment may increase the chances of the child's honest, if rage-filled, expressions of his underlying sentiments and perceptions towards caretakers, specifically towards the foster parents.

In treatment of Barry, some increase in verbalization was produced in verbally confrontive psychotherapy sessions with the therapist and one or both foster parents present. Prior to the onset of these sessions, the foster parents had been prepared by the therapist, without Barry present, to write down situations during the week in which Barry could have been expected to be angry with them. Of course, Barry's automatic response in those situations had been to smile at the foster parents, while failing to voice any anger at them.

What follows is a sample of how verbally confrontive psychotherapy drew out some verbalizations from Barry, which seemed to reflect his underlying negative working model. (Note: the reason for using a confrontive rather than non-directive approach is that the negative working model is stubbornly hidden from all adults. More orthodox mental health approaches, such as play therapy, rarely break through the resistance of the seriously attachment-disordered child to reveal the distorted, negative working model and to expose the depth of anger and other emotion which lies behind the child's smiling veneer.)

In the following excerpt, Barry is pressed aggressively by the therapist and the foster mother to admit openly to the anger felt towards his caretakers. In doing that Barry also reveals his previously hidden negative views about the world.

* * * * *

Foster mother: *"Barry told me that he had not taken the last three donuts out of the pantry, but I knew he was lying. He was the only child left home."*

Barry: (smiling and speaking softly) *"I didn't take it, Mom. One of the other kids took the donuts before church. Why don't you believe me?"*

Therapist: *"How can you expect us to believe you when you lie so much,*

Barry? You don't tell us the truth and you don't tell us your real feelings.''

Barry: (almost inaudibly) *"I do too."*

Therapist: *"I can't hear you. Tell me again."*

Barry: (somewhat above a whisper) *"Yes, I do too."*

Therapist: *"You do what, Barry? Speak up!"*

Barry: (more loudly, but still smiling) *"I tell the truth."*

Therapist: *"Then, why are you smiling now when you are angry?"*

Barry: (dropping his smile) *"I'm not smiling."*

Therapist: *"And you are still angry at us, aren't you?"*

Barry: (smiling again) *"Not really angry, no."*

Therapist: *"Then, why are you smiling again. You shouldn't smile at us when you're mad."*

Barry: (in frustration) *"Then, leave me alone and you won't have to see me smile!"*

Therapist: *"How can we leave you alone, when you lie to us?"*

Barry: (with no smile and anger apparent in his voice) *"Why shouldn't I lie, nobody listens to me anyway!"*

Foster Mother: *"We want to listen to you, Barry, but you never tell us what you want."*

Barry: (angrily) *"You don't have time to listen to me. You've got Timmy (their birth child) to listen to!"*

Therapist: (enthusiastically and positively) *"Now you're talking, Barry! Good job! Now let's talk about how you always hide in your room and won't talk to anyone."*

* * * * *

As might be clear in the therapy sample above, the negative working model finally emerges, as Barry speaks about how "nobody listens" and about how another child is more important to the parents. A verbally confrontive approach was used with Barry, after it was determined that he would not open up in more conventional, non-directive psychotherapy.

Obviously, Barry held many cynical expectations about caretakers and about himself. Barry felt no confidence in parent figures nor in his ability to derive what he needed in his relationships to them. He felt impotent and unimportant and very enraged. However, due to his harsh upbringing and his resultant distrust of fearsome adults, Barry would not express his negative feelings directly towards caretakers. Instead, he would habitually act-out towards younger children, while avoiding confrontation with adults. In general, he did not share true thoughts and feelings with any adults, nor did he ask for what he wanted or negotiate for what he needed.

The confrontive approach described above can often be very useful with children like Barry. Working closely with the foster parents, the therapist identifies in the child's daily life the behaviors which signal an underlying negative working model. Stealing, for example, in many foster children suggests the perception of caretakers as stingy, ungiving, and neglectful. The child's view of himself, if he chronically steals, is that he must take what is never freely given to him. Knowing what specific behavior problems have emerged in the foster home, the therapist presses the child to voice what has previously been, for him, unspeakable. The behavior or problems have expressed the underlying negative working model, though in an often confusing, many times destructive way.

As seen in the therapy excerpt above, the therapist confronts Barry's acting-out and presses him to verbalize what he really feels. At first, this approach might seem taunting, insensitive, and even non-therapeutic to some therapists and foster parents. And indeed, the approach is inappropriate with less troubled children — psychoneurotic or situationally disturbed youngsters, for example. However, with many children who have been abused, neglected, and abandoned to the point of developing significant attachment disorders, verbal confrontation is indispensable. (It should be noted that the therapist in these sessions must mix in confrontation with humor, warmth, and a sense of sincere concern for the child.)

As seen above, verbal confrontation serves to challenge acting-out during the child's week in the foster home, and it also challenges the acting-out (or defenses) which the child shows in the therapy session. For instance, the therapist confronted Barry's almost constant, incongruous smiling. With verbal confrontation the negative working model emerges in vivid detail. The child's hidden picture of the world shows itself. Perhaps for the first time the child articulates, though primitively, his view of things, his grievances, his rage. As a formerly maltreated child, he cannot always be expected to vocalize these buried sentiments without a big therapeutic push. That push can be provided by verbal confrontation, especially when used along with containment procedures.

(Note: foster parents can be quite instrumental in helping the child voice the unspeakable in the home. Foster parents can focus on situations in the home wherein a foster child fails to express normal levels of frustration, anger, jealousy, etc. The foster parent, rather than letting the moment pass unnoticed, can press the child to make some statements about his negative feelings in those situations. Of course, with the most disturbed, attachment-disordered children, resistance is strong. Acting-out will continue unabated, all the while the child vigorously denies feeling any anger whatsoever. Verbally confrontive approaches may be needed to break through the staunch resistance of such children. (It should be pointed out here that skilled mental health professionals can be quite helpful to foster parents who are trying to decide how and with which children to use verbally confrontive approaches in the home.))

The objective in using verbal confrontation is to elicit from the child statements which reflect his underlying negative working model. If the negative working model goes unverbalized, it is much more likely to appear in conduct problems, i.e. the language of the attachment-disordered child. The child remains bitterly impotent, secretly rage-filled, and forever isolated from those who could provide for him. Underneath it all, the negative working model continues unchanged. Healthier attachment relationships are thwarted by that model and ultimately the foster placement may be jeopardized.

3. Fostering Negotiating Skills.

As discussed in Chapter One, the typical infant/child passes through four stages on the road to normal attachment formation. This culminates in the stage of "partnership." This final stage of attachment, which is thought to span a life-time, involves the child's communication and negotiation of needs, wants, conflicts, and differences with caretakers and others.

As might be expected, the maltreated foster child's attachment process, being abnormal, has not developed to the point of a partnership. The attachment-disordered, foster child typically does not negotiate needs, wants, conflicts with anyone. More characteristically, he resorts to solitary attempts at either meeting his needs and wants or at negotiating conflicts.

Disturbed foster children may avoid making direct, assertive requests of caretakers. At the dinner table, for example, they may not ask for seconds, but later in the evening forage for food surreptitiously while their foster parents sleep. If they are sick or injured, these foster children may not even mention this or may not approach the caretaker for help and comfort. If they are frustrated with the foster parents over some perceived grievance, they will not voice their protest, but instead engage in some vengeful behavior at a later time. Barry, for example, who smiled constantly to cover up angry feelings, had been systematically gouging expensive furniture with his pocket knife in places where the foster parents would not immediately notice. The pattern which emerged was one in which Barry acted destructively towards foster parent's possessions, whenever he felt slighted, passed over, or ignored. (Barry appeared to lack much insight into when these feelings emerged, and likewise he seemed unwilling and unable to clearly vocalize when he felt aggrieved. Additionally, he was essentially too passive and non-assertive to make his poorly understood needs known to others. In essence then, he seemed chronically frustrated and embittered with caretakers who could not recognize and address his needs.)

The third component of therapeutic intervention with Barry centered on building negotiation skills. This necessitated some basic work on simple identification of feelings, needs, and wants. Additionally, Barry required prompting and coaching in vocalizing his feelings, needs, and wants. A sample of psychotherapeutic intervention, with the help of the foster parents, follows:

* * * * *

Therapist: *"We know you carved up the piano. So, don't tell us you didn't do it. We just want to know why you did it."*

Barry: *"I didn't do it because I was mad."*

Therapist: *"Don't you like pianos or something?"*

Barry: *"It's not that. I just wasn't thinking."*

Therapist: (to the Foster Mother) *"Doesn't Timmy take the piano?"*

Foster Mother: *"Well, actually, I am teaching Timmy the piano myself."*

Therapist: (to Barry sarcastically) *"I bet you love to see them sitting at the piano together, don't you?"*

Barry: (in an unusually honest moment) *"I hate it."*

Therapist: (to Barry) *"Maybe you would like some attention from your mother (i.e. foster mother) too. Is that right?"*

Barry: *"I don't know."*

Therapist: *"Come on, Barry...you want some attention too...Right?"*

Barry: *"Maybe."*

Therapist: *"Maybe? Be honest, Barry. You want attention too."*

Barry: (shrugging silently)

Therapist: *"Barry, all kids want attention, don't they?...Don't they, Barry? Don't they?"*

Barry: (grudgingly) *"I guess."*

Therapist: (pressing) *"You guess! Come on, Barry. I want you to say you want attention. Admit it. Say it, 'I want attention.'"*

Barry: *"Do I have to?"*

Therapist: *"Yes. Say it now."*

Barry (reluctantly, monotonously): *"I want attention."*

Therapist: *"Louder, with feeling, Barry!"*

Barry (increasingly testy, sarcastic): *"I want attention."*

Therapist: *"You can do better than that. Louder, Barry."*

Barry: *"I don't want to!"*

Therapist: *"That's too bad. You have to do this right...Say it louder."*

Barry: *"I want attention."*

Therapist: *"Even louder!"*

Barry (growing more impatient): *"God...I want attention!"*

Therapist: *"Better! Now look at your foster mother and say it to her."*

Barry (looking in her direction): *"I want attention."*

Therapist: *"Look into her eyes and say it again, louder."*

* * * * *

What came out after this encounter was that Barry would skulk around the foster home without making his needs known to anyone. His assumptions about himself and his caretakers effectively prevented him from even asking for what he wanted. Indeed, he really had a hazy picture of what his wants were at any given time. Nonetheless, he spent a great deal of time feeling resentful, envious, jealous and bitterly helpless to do anything about it, except to act out vengefully.

Through many, frequent psychotherapeutic encounters similar to the sample provided above, Barry was stimulated to voice thoughts, feelings, wants and needs which were heretofore unspeakable and unspoken. (And in the foster home, Barry was coached, prompted, humored, and pressured to state what he wanted rather than to hide in his room. We will see ahead how the foster mother's efforts at home augmented psychotherapeutic approaches in the office.) In effect, his earliest experiences of maltreatment had "conditioned" him to avoid overt expressions of needs, thoughts, etc. His negative working model prevented him from seeing himself as anything other than unsafe, worthless, and impotent; and it kept him from viewing caretakers as anything other than unresponsive, unreliable, and dangerous. By pressing Barry into speaking and acting differently, the therapist allowed this child to experience himself as safe, valuable, and capable and his caretakers as responsive, reliable, and harmless. This new experience would contradict the negative working model. As you might expect, countless experiences would be needed to alter the negative working model even slightly.

(It is beyond the scope of this book to present a full range of therapeutic approaches to provide the child with negotiating skills. However, the example given above gives a flavor of the way in which the therapist can stimulate new behavior which can meet with different reactions from the foster parents. Pressing the child in this way thwarts the reenactment process, puts the foster parents in a proactive rather than reactive position, and ultimately challenges the child's negative working model.)

To augment the psychotherapy process, the focus in the foster home centered upon Barry's making overt, direct requests for one-on-one attention from the foster mother. If he did not come to the foster mother on a daily basis with at least one request, she would go to him and force the request out of him in a playful but firm way, as we see below.

* * * * *

Mrs. T., the foster mother, yelled out loudly, "Barry, if you don't come here now and tell me what you want from me, I'll come after you!" After there was no response, Mrs. T. sought Barry in his bedroom, where he was lying face down with a scowl on his face. Sitting on top of him on the bed, she began to tickle him playfully and in lilting tones said, "Tell me you want to do something with me!" She continued to sit on him and tickle. as he wriggled and eventually blurted out, "Okay, do something with me." "I already am.

I'm tickling you,'' she teased him. Barry seemed to grow increasingly frustrated, and finally yelled, ''Get off and I'll tell you.'' When Mrs. T. got off, Barry resumed his scowling, but did not say anything further. Twenty minutes later, after Mrs. T. had been teasing and tickling Barry again, he finally made a serious request. ''Take me to the pet store, then.'' Although he made the request bluntly and almost grudgingly, Mrs. T. knew that the request was heartfelt, because Barry loved animals, though he would mistreat them when upset. Later that day, Barry and Mrs. T. took a drive to a local pet shop.

* * * * *

As in the case of Barry, treatment of other attachment-disordered foster children must focus on building negotiating skills. The negative working model renders the foster child skeptical of his ability to negotiate with caretakers for the purpose of meeting his needs. A host of problems ensue, when the child feels that parents can or will not help him meet his needs, and when he feels that he is powerless to get them to help him.

4. Promoting Positive Encounters.

Maltreated foster children often send mixed messages to foster parents about caretaking. Negative behaviors, i.e. conduct problems, invite increases in parenting, caretaking, negative-attention, etc. That is, the parent feels instinctively protective, alarmed, or displeased by the foster child's conduct problems and is drawn towards intervening as caretaker. For instance, when the child steals, the parent feels compelled to confront, investigate, question the child, seek out the truth, obtain an apology, express his disappointment in the child, and mete out consequences for the misdeed. Thus, the stealing heightens parental involvement, though it may be negative. Indeed, most of the maltreated child's conduct problems (see Appendix) seem to insure a certain, perhaps constant, level of negative attention from caretakers. Often, children who have been abused and/or neglected develop pervasively negative ways of inviting increased caretaking. In the process, they may, in effect, invite more abuse. Almost certainly, they receive responses from parents (i.e. the foster parents) which reinforce the negative working model; they have become accustomed to the negative mode of interacting with caretakers and reenact earlier patterns which produce the familiar parenting reactions.

As mentioned above, countless negative interactions with caretakers culminate in the formation of the negative working model. The expectation about parent figures is that they cannot be trusted to give nurturance and attention voluntarily and consistently. They must, in line with the negative working model, be maneuvered, manipulated, and forced into giving care. The expectation of negative, conflictual interactions with parents becomes unshakable. Ironically, the child may perceive positive, nurturing, harmonious interactions with parent figures as frighteningly unusual and unacceptable.

Returning to the case of Barry, the foster parents found him to be a "cold fish," i.e. avoidant, refusing of affectionate overtures, withdrawn, and phobic of physical touch and verbal compliments. Though he was indisputably a very needy child emotionally, Barry seemed to reject compulsively what he lacked most, i.e. positive caretaking. As we see below, the psychologist set about trying to alter Barry's negative working model and at the same time, to increase Barry's openness to positive caretaking.

*　*　*　*　*

In a relatively short time, Barry's conduct problems (as well as his general mode of interacting or not interacting) had taken their toll on the foster parents. In short order, these parents had begun to recoil self-protectively from Barry. Though they felt few abusive impulses towards him, his thorough withdrawal from them prompted them to consider placing him elsewhere (i.e. the urge to reject). Nevertheless, though Barry was quite withdrawn — hiding in his room, shirking hugs, avoiding family gatherings, refusing first aid from family members if he were hurt, and refusing to talk and answer questions — several behavior problems seemed to invite negative parental behavior. Stealing food, sneaky destruction of property, and aggressive behavior towards the younger children placed the foster parents in the position of intervening punitively with Barry. They, in fact, reported feeling "locked into" a largely unfulfilling, thankless role with a child who refused their positive attention, while demanding negative involvement.

In the short run, the task for the psychologist here was to assist the foster family in finding a way to "reach" Barry, (i.e. to engage him with more positive caretaking via by-passing his conduct problems). (The long range goal was to alter the negative working model, and thus to eliminate barriers to healthier attachment formation.) As luck would have it, Barry had head lice, which he had passed onto other foster family members. Every two days the family administered shampoos to each other with Kwell, an anti-lice scalp treatment. Though Barry was generally "tactilely defensive," i.e. refusing touch, holding, physical affection from the foster parents, he would submit to regular shampoos by the foster mother. The psychologist asked the foster mother to gradually increase the frequency and duration of the shampoos. The shampoos were to become increasingly luxurious and were to expand to facial massage, hair brushing, etc. After two months Barry was receiving daily shampoos, brushings, facials, and neck rubs from the foster mother. At his most relaxed at those moments, Barry openly accepted this very specific parenting.

* * * * *

Over time and through many encounters (both in psychotherapy sessions and in the foster home) such as those described above, Barry's conduct problems diminished. Along with that, the foster parents reported a reduction in their desire to reject Barry or to have him removed from the home. Indeed, they stated that he seemed increasingly part of their family; and he had become more approachable and more positively engaging. In a word, Barry had become likeable.

Barry, by the age of eleven, was considerably less withdrawn and avoidant. His lying and food stealing had all but disappeared. That is, those problems were occasional; and Barry would admit to having stolen, after he was confronted with the deed. In addition, other problems had subsided. Barry slept through the night without roaming the house in the dark. He had not set a fire (or even played with matches) for several months — a personal best for him. Further, Barry was no longer destructive to the foster parents' possessions, nor was he physically hurtful towards the younger children in the home, though he often complained about them to the foster parents. Barry only rarely seemed insincere, and he smiled, when he felt happy — not when he was anxious, angry or deceitful. In all, his major conduct problems had been contained.

On the whole, Barry had become more verbally expressive of his feelings, opinions, wants, and needs. He could more easily confront, disagree with, complain to, and make demands upon the foster parents. (In short, he had learned to negotiate.) Interestingly, the foster parents reported that Barry acted more like their own children. That is, he seemed more natural, feisty, comfortable, and at times, obnoxious. Oddly, they felt assured and even flattered by the "obnoxious" side which Barry had revealed to them. It made him at times more challenging to deal with, but also gave him some dimension, some genuineness that he had lacked before treatment.

Finally, the foster parents stated that Barry had begun to attach to them and vice versa. A mutual affection and committment seemed apparent in psychotherapy sessions. Barry seemed to invite, initiate, and accept intimate exchanges with the foster parents. He seemed to expect acceptance from them and to feel confident in his ability to derive what he needed from them. Evidentally, his negative working model had been substantially altered.

Concluding Remarks.

All too commonly, foster parents report that the attachment-disordered child has failed to become a part of their family, i.e. that he has resisted incorporation into the home, even though he has been in long-term or permanent foster placement. This child can often find ways of undermining closeness, sabotaging attachment formation, and torpedoing the stability of the placement. Just when the family seems to be making some gains, the child "messes up." In general the child is giving his caretakers a "stiff arm," keeping them at a safe, familiar distance. He actively, or sometimes passively, withdraws and isolates himself from truly intimate, fulfilling, healing relationships.

Although there are many less disturbed foster children who may respond to a "laissez-faire" (i.e. hands-off) approach, avoidant, attachment-disordered youngsters might remain withdrawn indefinitely and perhaps permanently, without active mental health and foster parent interventions. Conduct problems, reenactment, and the underlying negative working model would conspire to spoil success without such intervention.

With some foster children the barriers to intimacy, nurturance and positive caretaking are seemingly insurmountable. These children might, due to severity of their attachment-disorder, obstinately resist the type of program which we have depicted herein for use with Barry. In such cases, more extreme mental health interventions may be necessary. Unfortunately, some attachment-disordered foster children require placement in residential treatment facilities or psychiatric hospitals, when conduct problems result in danger to self or others. However, with all but the most severely attachment-disordered children, the unorthodox mental health interventions described above can have a measurable, therapeutic impact on the disturbed foster child and on his negative working model.

References

Ainsworth, Mary D. Salter; Blehar, Mary; Waters, Everett; and Wall, Sally. *Patterns of Attachment: A Psychological Study of the Strange Situation.* New Jersey: Lawrence Erlbaum Associates, 1978.

Anthony, E. James and Cohler, Bertram, J. (Eds.) *The Invulnerable Child.* New York: Guilford Press, 1987.

Bates, John and Bayles, Kathryn. "Attachment and the Development of Behavior Problems," In Jay Belsky and Teresa Nezworski (Eds.) *Clinical Implications of Attachment.* New Jersey: Lawrence Erlbaum Associates, 1988.

Belsky, Jay and Nezworski, Teresa. *Clinical Implications of Attachment.* New Jersey: Lawrence Erlbaum Associates, 1988.

Bowlby, John. *Attachment and Loss. Volume I: Attachment.* New York: Basic Books, 1969.

Bowlby, John. *Attachment and Loss. Volume II: Separation.* New York: Basic Books, 1973.

Brazelton, T. Berry and Cramer, Bertrand G. *The Earliest Relationship.* New York: Addison-Wesley Publishing, 1990.

Bretherton, Inge; Ridgeway, Doreen; and Cassidy, Jude. "Assessing Internal Working Models of the Attachment Relationship: An Attachment Story Completion Task for Three-Year-Olds," In Mark T. Greenberg; Dante Cicchetti; and E. Mark Cummings (Eds.), *Attachment in the Preschool Years.* Chicago: University of Chicago Press, 1990.

Cline, Foster. *Understanding and Treating the Severely Disturbed Child.* Evergreen, CO: Evergreen Consultants, 1979.

Delaney, Richard. *Attachment Problems in Children.* Unpublished manuscript. 1990.

Dollard, John and Miller, Neal. *Personality and Psychotherapy.* New York: McGraw-Hill, 1950.

Fahlberg, Vera Colburn. *Attachment and Separation.* Lansing, Michigan: Office of Family and Youth Services, 1979.

Fraiberg, Selma. *Clinical Studies in Infant Mental Health.* New York: Basic Books, 1980.

Greenberg, Mark T.; Cicchetti; Dante; and Cummings, E. Mark (Eds). *Attachment in the Preschool Years.* Chicago: University of Chicago Press, 1990.

Group for the Advancement of Psychiatry. *Psychological Disorders in Childhood.* New York: GAP, 1966.

Kagan, Jerome. *The Nature of the Child.* New York: Basic Books, 1984.

Magid, Ken and McKelvey, Carole. *High Risk: Children Without A Conscience.* New York: Bantam Books, 1987

Mahler, Margaret; Pine, Fred; and Bergman, Anni. *The Psychological Birth of the Human Infant.* New York: Basic Books, 1975.

Lieberman, Alicia and Pawl, Jaree. "Clinical Applications of Attachment Theory," In Jay Belsky and Teresa Nezworski (Eds.) *Clinical Implications of Attachment.* New Jersey: Lawrence Erlbaum Associates, 1988.

Main, Mary and Solomon, Judith. "Procedures for Identifying Infants as Disorganized/Disoriented During the Ainsworth Strange Situation," In Mark T. Greenberg; Dante Cicchetti; and E. Mark Cummings (Eds.), *Attachment in the Preschool Years.* Chicago: University of Chicago Press, 1990.

Main, Mary and Hesse, Erik. "Parents' Unresolved Traumatic Experiences Are Related to Infant Disorganized Attachment Status: Is Frightened and/or Frightening Parental Behavior the Linking Mechanism?" In Mark T. Greenberg; Dante Cicchetti; and E. Mark Cummings (Eds.) *Attachment in the Preschool Years.* Chicago: University of Chicago Press, 1990.

Masterson, James. *Treatment of the Borderline Adolescent.* New York: Wiley-Interscience, 1972.

Pearson, Gerald. *A Handbook of Child Psychoanalysis.* New York: Basic Books, 1968.

Pound, Andrea. "Attachment and Maternal Depression," In Colin Murray Parkes and Joan Stevenson-Hinde (Eds.), *Attachment in Human Behavior.* New York: Basic Books, 1982.

Schneider-Rosen, Karen. "The Developmental Reorganization of Attachment Relationships: Guidelines for Classification Beyond Infancy," In Mark T. Greenberg; Dante Cicchetti; and E. Mark Cummings (Eds.), *Attachment in the Preschool Years.* Chicago: University of Chicago Press, 1990.

Speltz, Matthew. "The Treatment of Preschool Conduct Problems: An Integration of Behavioral and Attachment Concepts," In Mark T. Greenberg; Dante Cicchetti; and E. Mark Cummings (Eds.), *Attachment in the Preschool Years.* Chicago: University of Chicago Press, 1990.

Spieker, Susan and Booth, Cathryn. "Maternal Antecedents of Attachment Quality," In Jay Belsky and Teresa Nezworski (Eds.) *Clinical Implications of Attachment.* New Jersey: Lawrence Erlbaum Associates, 1988.

Stroufe, L. Alan. "The Role of Infant-Caregiver Attachment in Development," In Jay Belsky and Teresa Nezworski (Eds.) *Clinical Implications of Attachment.* New Jersey: Lawrence Erlbaum Associates, 1988.

McDermott, John; Fraiberg, Selma; and Harrison, Saul I. "Residential Treatment of Children: The Utilization of Transference Behavior, "In Stella Chess and Alexander Thomas (Eds.) *Annual Progress in Child Psychiatry and Child Development.* New York: Brunner/Mazel, 1969.

Wiltse, Kermit T. "Foster Care — An Overview," In Joan Laird and Ann Hartman (Eds.), *A Handbook of Child Welfare.* New York: The Free Press, 1985.

Related Publications

Cicchetti, Dante; Cummings, E. Mark; Greenberg, Mark T.; and Marvin, Robert S. "An Organizational Perspective on Attachment Beyond Infancy: Implications for Theory, Measurement, and Research," In Mark T. Greenberg; Dante Cicchetti; and E. Mark Cummings (Eds.), *Attachment in the Preschool Years.* Chicago: University of Chicago Press, 1990.

Crittenden, Patricia. "Relationships at Risk," In Jay Belsky and Teresa Nezworski (Eds.) *Clinical Implications of Attachment.* New Jersey: Lawrence Rerlbaum Associates, 1988.

Diagnostic and Statistics Manual III-Revised. Washington, D.C.: American Psychiatric Association, 1987.

Erikson, Erik H. *Childhood and Society.* New York: Norton, 1963.

Fanshel, David. "Status Changes of Children in Foster Care," In Stella Chess and Alexander Thomas (Eds.), *Annual Progress in Child Psychiatry and Child Development,* 1977.

Goldstein, Joseph; Freud, Anna; and Solnit, Albert J. *Beyond the Best Interests of the Child.* New York: Free Press, 1973.

Greenberg, Mark and Speltz, Matthew. "Attachment and the Ontogeny of Conduct Problems," In Jay Belsky and Teresa Nezworksi (Eds.) *Clinical Implications of Attachment.* New Jersey: Lawrence Erlbaum Associates, 1988.

Greenspan, Stanley I. and Lieberman, Alicia F. "A Clinical Approach to Attachment," In Jay Belsky and Teresa Nezworski (Eds.) *Clinical Implications of Attachment.* New Jersey: Lawrence Erlbaum Associates, 1988.

Jewett, Claudia. *Adopting the Older Child.* Boston: The Harvard Common Press, 1978.

Kempe, C. Henry and Helfer, Ray E. *Helping the Battered Child and His Family.* Philadelphia: Lippincott, 1972.

Minuchin, Salvador. *Families and Family Therapy.* Cambridge: Harvard University Press, 1974.

Parkes, Colin Murray and Stevenson-Hinde, Joan (Eds.). *The Place of Attachment in Human Behavior.* New York: Basic Books, 1982.

Redl, Fritz and Wineman, David. *Children Who Hate.* New York: Free Press, 1951.

Rose, Thomas and Rose, Dorothea Wend. "Adoption, Foster Care, and Group Homes for Handicapped Children," In Ann Hartman and Joan Laird (Eds.), *A Handbook of Child Welfare.* New York: Free Press, 1985.

Sameroff, Arnold and Emde, Robert. *Relationship Disturbance in Early Childhood.* New York: Basic Books, 1989.

Sperling, Melitta. *The Major Neuroses and Behavior Disorders in Children.* New York: Aronson, 1974.

Spitz, Rene. *The First Year of Life.* New York: International Universities Press, 1965.

Swire, Margaret and Kavaler, Florence. "The Health Status of Foster Children," *Child Welfare,* Volume 56, 635-653, 1977.

Whittaker, James T. "Group and Institutional Care — An Overview," In Ann Hartman and Joan Laird (Eds.), *A Handbook of Child Welfare.* New York: Free Press, 1985.

Williams, Gertrude and Money, John. (Eds.) *Traumatic Abuse and Neglect of Children at Home.* Baltimore: John Hopkins University Press, 1980.

Woolf, Gaetana DiBerto. "An Outlook for Foster Care in the United States," *Child Welfare,* Volume LXIX, No. 1, Jan/Feb, 1990.

Appendix: Symptoms

Conduct Problems of Attachment-Disorders in Foster Children.

Attachment-disordered, maltreated foster children manifest a variety of symptoms — many of which are conduct problems — in placement. They fall into seven symptom clusters or categories: sadism/violence; disordered eating; counterfeit emotionality; compulsive lying and kleptomania; sexual obsessions; passive/aggression; and defective conscience. The exact symptom picture will depend upon (1) the severity of the disturbance, (2) the age of the child, (3) the child's individual history, and other factors. These symptoms and conduct problems typically stem from the child's negative working model (see Chapter Two), i.e. his pessimistic view of himself and caretakers.

Before turning to a discussion of symptoms, I might add that those listed here are most commonly seen in school-aged, maltreated, attachment-disordered foster children, although preschoolers and adolescents share some of the same symptoms. The children who show many or most of the symptoms and conduct problems listed below have been diagnosed by some clinicians as "unattached" (Cline, 1979; Magid, 1987). These are children who have been exposed to the most horrendous physical abuse and neglect, and they must be distinguished from those children who have experienced minor forms of disruptions (and much less maltreatment) during the attachment process (Brazelton and Cramer, 1990). Early-on in their lives these children might have been Type A, C, or D infants (Main and Solomon, 1990), although the exact connection between early quirks in attachment and later "unattachment" remains relatively unknown.

The following list is not meant to encompass all the symptoms which attachment-disordered children show by school age. Indeed, there are undoubtedly many attachment-disordered children who are less disturbed and less angry than the group described below (Delaney, 1990). Those children of less disturbance might be expected to show greater signs of insecurity, dependence, phobia, and fears of being alone. They would be more likely called "overanxiously attached" (Bowlby, 1973; Delaney, 1990).

Finally, not all children showing the symptoms described herein are attachment-disordered, as defined in this book. Many of these symptoms can be explained by other conditions than an attachment-disorder, for example, clinical depression, attention deficit hyperactivity disorder, etc. The most accurate assessments of attachment-disorders will rest on more than a mere tally of symptoms.

Sadism/Violence

The deep rage felt by the attachment-disordered child often finds expression in the symptom of sadism and violence. This symptom category includes such behaviors as cruelty to animals and children; vandalism/destructiveness towards property; assaultive and combative behavior; self-injurious behavior; and fire-setting. In all of these behavior problems, we find evidence of the child's hidden fury.

Cruelty to Animals and Children.

The attachment-disordered child often cruelly victimizes helpless animals and children. At times, his angry actions burst out explosively, without forethought. At other times, the rage emerges in premeditated ways as in the following case example, where it assumes a very sadistic form.

* * * * *

Tommy, an attachment-disordered twelve-year-old foster child, specialized in inflicting pain onto animals, wild and tame alike. On one occasion, Tommy buried a puppy alive, while threatening to do the same thing to the young children who witnessed his actions. On another, Tommy doused some blackbirds with gasoline and then set them on fire as he let them go.

* * * * *

An oft-reported symptom, sadism (or violent behavior), signals not only a negative working model and disordered attachment but past exposure to physical abuse. Tommy, for example, absorbed a great deal of physical abuse from his cruel alcoholic father. As with other maltreated, attachment-disordered children, Tommy's sadism springs from a reservoir of stored anger. Commonly such anger focuses on helpless creatures. Of course, some essentially normal children treat animals with harshness. Boys, for example, will hunt small animals with bows and arrows, and they might pull the wings from insects. These behaviors may be a sign of the child conquering his fears of the animal kingdom. Much of that behavior, when not compulsive, may be expectable in the school-aged child. However, sadistic treatment of pets, usually done in solitary, is often a tell-tale sign of serious emotional problems. This pain-inflicting behavior may act to displace anger. That is, the child, who may have been the helpless target of a more powerful individual's wrath, punishes helpless creatures in turn. Dominance over helpless animals may reduce the child's sense of helplessness in the face of cruel treatment from parents, older siblings, etc. The child learns to treat the helpless in the same cruel fashion in which he himself has been treated. In so doing, he models his behavior after those who have abused him. An unfortunate pet becomes the undeserved, but safe target for anger which originated in a relationship to an abusive parent. One attachment-disordered, adoptive boy was avoided by all the family pets. This boy routinely stomped on the dog's feet and once hit it over the head with a lead pipe; this same child also attempted to string-up a cat by the neck, and decapitated several pet hamsters and blamed it on the family cat.

Smaller children also fall prey to the simmering rage of the attachment-disordered child. Mysteriously, infants left with these children cry more often. Small children cry over injuries in which the attachment-disordered child denies involvement.

Interestingly, maltreated foster children are often unable to express anger towards the adult world directly. Some of these children may consciously view adults as fearsome and dangerous, and thus suppress anger felt towards them. Other children may be unconsciously angry (the negative working model) towards caretakers, while consciously feeling quite positive towards them. In either case, these children often vent anger on safer targets such as animals and younger children.

Vandalism/Destructiveness.

In vandalism and destructiveness, the attachment-disordered child unleashes his violent anger towards inanimate objects. This behavior signals the presence of a deep reservoir of rage, which may never or seldom appear interpersonally (especially towards adult caretakers).

* * * * *

Jeremy, a quiet, anemic looking ten-year-old, had led a group of younger boys into the local elementary school after hours. With his encouragement, they totally ransacked the school, smashing up typewriters, breaking Apple computer screens, flooding the bathrooms, and writing misspelled graffiti on the walls. School personnel were completely shocked by Jeremy's involvement, as he was a "model student." The foster mother was less bewildered, since Jeremy had frequently damaged objects in the home behind her back.

* * * * *

Vandalism and other forms of destructiveness often signal the presence of underlying, often repressed anger, associated attachment disorders, and a negative working model. Similar to sadistic behavior towards living things, destructive acts provide an avenue for expression of otherwise contained anger. Often times, the foster child may be quite passive and compliant towards adults, all the while concealing the rage within. He is often simply afraid of the adult world, to which he relates with passivity and non-assertion. Rather than dealing with his anger directly with adults — as the normal child will — this child secretly harbors rage which eventually emerges in destructiveness, vandalism, and/or in other oblique ways. In the home, vandalism may take many forms;

for example, the child might secretly bore holes in the walls, disfigure furniture or flush large objects down the toilet. At times, his anger bursts out publicly, when he breaks out windows, tears up his room, or throws a toy through the television screen during a temper tantrum. However, public, interpersonal displays of anger may be the exception, in that with many attachment-disordered children destructiveness typically remains secret.

Assaultive Behavior Towards Adults.

In some rare foster children, the underlying rage erupts in periodic physical assaults towards adults. (Most attachment-disordered children will avoid any physical confrontation with caretakers whatsoever, while others are combative.) Some children, who are typically more passive-aggressive and manipulative, become increasingly attack-oriented when firm controls are placed on their behavior, perhaps for the first time in their lives.

Generally speaking assaultive behavior may be prompted by: (1) the adult's attempt to limit, confront or discipline the child and (2) the child's displacement of anger from other areas or other times of his life onto a "safe" adult (i.e. the foster parent). Assaultive behavior can assume a variety of forms, such as: biting, scratching, pinching, pushing, spitting, hitting, pulling hair, kicking, throwing objects, butting with the head, and brandishing of a weapon.

* * * * *

Bespectacled and thin, Ricardo, at age ten, looked more like a miniature college professor than dangerous assailant. Yet, he was well known to the school staff as a potential threat to student and, in particular, to personnel safety. Chronically abused in the past by his brothers and a series of stepfathers, Robert vented his anger in the caring, harmless school environment. Showing much fewer conduct problems in the foster home, Robert displaced his mounting anger onto school staff who attempted to contain his acting-out behavior. Especially after week-end visits to the home of his birth mother and stepfather, Robert came back to school with seething anger. He seemed to provoke adults more than children. Robert, sometimes when asked to do minor things, would explode violently. He had, in his younger years, bitten and scratched staff. Now, at ten, he would throw objects at the teachers and, on one occasion, he hit a teacher's aide over the head with baseball bat.

* * * * *

As mentioned above, attachment-disordered children may erupt with physical assault against the adult, when there is an attempt to limit, confront, or discipline. With foster children who have, in the past, had little or no supervision or parental guidance, any adult control evokes rage. The child has often refused to surrender control to adults who are viewed as abusive, erratic, over or under-involved. (The child's working model here would contain expectations about adult caretakers which were totally negative. In cases like these the child may be consciously angry towards all caretakers or may idealize some and devalue others.) Oftentimes, attachment-disordered children have, in effect, raised themselves, having been exposed to inadequate/abusive parents. They have, over time, developed ways of avoiding, manipulating, resisting, and outsmarting the adults around them. (Again, speaking from the vantage point of the child's internal working model, he would be expected to view parent figures as either unresponsive and neglectful, abusive and dangerous, or a combination of both.) When school personnel (or foster parents) attempt to intervene with discipline or supervision, the child attempts to avoid, manipulate, resist, and outsmart. If his old tactics fail to work due to consistency and confrontation of the school staff, the child feels backed into the corner, psychologically speaking. His assaultive behavior may emerge in response to feeling cornered.

Self-injurious Behavior.

Although rage is more commonly directed externally towards persons or things, the occasional attachment-disordered child directs destructive impulses towards himself and his own possessions. These children behave in self-destructive, self-injurious ways or they destroy their own belongings. They might be seen as more masochistic than sadistic, often hurt themselves and may be accident-prone as well.

* * * * *

Doreen, a sullen seven-year-old, foster girl, stood silently beside Mrs. S., her foster mother, who held a large, full Hefty bag in her hand. Dramatically, she dumped the contents onto the floor: a tangle of torn underwear, shredded pants, and tops ripped in half. Doreen had reportedly destroyed ninety percent of her new school clothes deliberately.

* * * * *

Children who are self-destructive (or destructive to their own belongings) behave intro-punitively. That is, they frequently direct anger towards themselves rather than towards others. The intro-punitive, foster child may also externalize his anger on occasion, only resorting to self-destructive behavior periodically. During those periods, the attachment-disordered child may head-bang, sometimes leaving bumps and bruises. Or, he may pick at sores until they bleed, or he might cut, burn, or tattoo his skin. (Cutting, burning or tattooing appear more often in disturbed adolescents. In the case of Doreen above, the child spared her own skin, while destroying her "second skin." Thus, her actions were not technically self-injurious, though her wardrobe suffered greatly.) Curiously, some children report a lack of pain during self-destructive acts. The child may often seem insensitive to pain, which would be experienced by others as excruciating. While some self-destructive behavior may symbolize the child's self-hatred, other self-destruction represents a bizarre form of stimulation in the child's otherwise under-stimulating world. Indeed, attachment-disordered children may be so psychologically jaded that only pain removes, at least for the moment, their psychic numbness.

Related to self-destructiveness, accident-proneness involves an attachment-disordered child who is fearless, reckless, and often injured. The normal reserve and common sense of the typical school-aged child escapes this foster child. He remains heedless of the dangers of fire, heights, or traffic. Historically, he had never internalized a sense of precaution, as we will see in the following case.

* * * * *

The caseworker brought in Bobby Jo, a burly, active three-year-old, female foster child, who wore casts on her left leg and right arm. Her right arm had been broken two weeks before, when she had fallen off the hood of a pick-up truck parked out front of her home. Her leg was fractured several days later when she attempted, unsuccessfully, to climb to the top of the garage roof. The caseworker reported that there had been little supervision in the home of Bobby Jo's biological parents. However, she added that the foster mother, an alert, experienced veteran caretaker, had recently found this girl — with arm and leg in a cast — attempting to climb out the second story window onto the roof. She was described as an "accident waiting to happen."

* * * * *

This accident-proneness in attachment-disordered children may derive from a combination of factors, such as the child's hyperactivity, impulsivity, and fearlessness (ironically, the same reckless child who shows no fear of physical hazards, may manifest extreme, constant wariness in interpersonal situations.)

Accident-proneness may also emerge out of a lack of parental supervision in an essentially unsafe environment. As in the case of Bobby Jo above, however, even with reasonable supervision in safe surroundings, certain children seem earmarked for injury. Many a foster mother has reported to me that when she lets go of the young child's hand, he will automatically dart out into traffic without looking where he is going. Others report that the child has absolutely no sense of danger. Frequently, the foster mother will report that she must watch the child constantly and cannot trust what he might do out of her sight.

These examples of accident-proneness point to underlying attachment problems. The children described herein often lack the normal child's internalized concern for self-preservation. Typically the normal child's parents have devoted hours towards correcting, protecting, and guiding the child through potentially harmful situations. With the attachment-disordered child, by contrast, we often find that the child has failed to internalize the concern for self-preservation from parent figures, either because the parent had no concern for the child or because the child put no stock in the parent's concerns. (Undoubtedly, the negative working model of the self is at work here. More specifically, the child may see himself as unwanted and worthless. Correspondingly, his efforts at self-preservation may be lessened, due to his lack of apparent value to the caretakers.)

Pyromania/Fire-setting.

Another form of violence, fire-setting (pyromania) is often symptomatic of the underlying anger in the attachment-disordered child. The fascination that some foster children have with fire and fire-setting far exceeds the normal curiosity shown by the average child. While it is unknown why these disturbed children become absorbed with firesetting, in general the symptom appears to be related to lack of supervision by parents and to aggressive feelings towards the world, as we see in the following case example.

* * * * *

Betsy, a very docile girl with attachment problems, sneaked down to the kitchen after the foster family had gone to bed, deliberately set a milk carton on the range, and then turned on the gas burners. Luckily the smoke detectors were set off by the fumes from the melting/burning carton.

* * * * *

With some foster children, like the docile girl above, we can trace fire-setting episodes to specific times when the child felt wronged, overlooked, or slighted. With other children, the anger is constant, and thus fire-setting emerges almost at random out of the general reservoir of rage. In the case of Betsy above, it was later established that the child had felt aggrieved earlier in the day, when the foster mother punished her for misbehavior. The fire-setting in this incident expressed anger in a primitive, potentially lethal fashion.

Disordered Eating

Disordered eating, the second symptom (category) in attachment disorders, includes behaviors such as stealing and hoarding of food, gorging, and food refusal. These behaviors suggest the attachment-disordered child's underlying feeling of deprivation and often indicate a history of emotional and physical neglect. Some disordered eating grows out of deep insensitivity on the parent's part towards the child's nutritional and/or psychological needs and wants. The working model underlying disordered eating is undoubtedly negative. The foster child likely views caretakers as stingy and ungiving, both physically and psychologically.

Stealing and Hoarding Food.

Given their histories of emotional and physical neglect, it is no wonder that many foster children steal and hoard food. Many of them come from homes where food was not readily and predictably available, often due to poverty. Other children report that their parents instituted a two-tiered approach to food: the parents ate relatively well, while the children had only table scraps. After placement in foster, these children continue to show age-old behaviors regarding food, even though it may be plentiful. Thus, foster families often must lock pantry and refrigerator doors to keep these children from eating them out of house and home. While some of the food is eaten on the spot, often in a midnight raid, other food stuffs are stockpiled for later use. Parents may later uncover secret caches of inedible food, rotting in the closet or between mattresses, as in the following example.

* * * * *

Ray Ann, a horribly overweight, ten-year-old girl had finally admitted to squirreling away large quantities of food in the garage, shed, and bedroom closet. According to the parents, Ray Ann was clearly obsessed with food. She talked about it constantly, reminiscing longingly about her favorite meals from the past. Before leaving for school each day, Ray Ann religiously would ask about the supper menu. On her bedroom wall she had constructed a collage of cut-outs from food magazines. Although her love affair with food was no secret, Ray Ann staunchly denied having stolen food from the cupboards, until she was finally caught in the wee hours of the morning carrying a large paper bag filled with Halloween candy meant for the whole family. It was then that the parents conducted a search of Ray Ann's bedroom. They were flabbergasted to find thirty cans of soup, several loaves of now stale bread, and miscellaneous silverware hidden between the mattresses.

* * * * *

Children with attachment problems often can be spotted by their atypical obsession with food. Some children steal and pack-rat all the food they can get their hands on, hiding secret booty in a variety of places. Others cannot wait to eat what they have laid their hands on and gorge ceaselessly until they vomit (see section on Gorging below). While many children, as might be expected, gravitate to cookies, candy sweets or junk foods, others forage for exotic delectables such as jellies, pickles, and hot peppers. Younger children — often previously diagnosed as failure to thrive — steal Fido's dog food, if left unattended. In those children who steal and hoard, gross neglect of physical and emotional needs undoubtedly has played a causal role.

In the case of adoptions of children from Viet Nam, South America and other third world countries, these attachment-disordered children, sometimes surviving on the streets, may have begged and stolen food. They never took food for granted. Not knowing when they might see any again, they likely over ate or hid it for later. In the new world, they retained their old attitudes about food and about the world.

Analogous to physically neglected children, some emotionally deprived youngsters become totally preoccupied with food. (It should be added here that, as with many of the symptoms described herein, there can be a number possible explanations for eating disorders, only one of which is an attachment disorder. Eating disorders, for example, have been long associated with clinical depression, which should checked out with many foster children.)

Gorging.

Food gorging is a frequently reported behavior problem in disturbed foster children. As you might expect, gorging often accompanies stealing and hoarding of food. Gorging, as observed in attachment-disordered children, greatly surpasses the "normal" gluttony seen in essentially healthy children. Eating-disordered foster children may gorge until they vomit, seemingly incapable of stopping once they have started.

Predictably, the attachment-disordered child's exposure to physical and emotional neglect propels him to gorge food, often to the point of physical pain and/or vomiting. His obsession with food drowns out the body sensations which signal fullness, as seen in the following case:

* * * * *

The mother and father were irate with their middle child, Mark, a scruffy, dishevelled nine-year-old boy with furtive eyes. They grilled him in front of me about the missing food. Although he proclaimed his innocence, they were convinced that he had secretly consumed (in one night) two boxes of cereal, three jars of jelly, and a full gallon of milk. In their anger, they had torn apart his room, only to find canned goods in the closet (under the dirty clothes), wrappers from stolen candy, and a stale loaf of bread pressed between the mattresses. In the night they had awakened to the sounds of Mark vomiting in the bathroom.

* * * * *

As with Mark, many foster children have an unholy obsession with food and will gorge whenever the chance arises. Some gorge at the dinner table, some gorge in private. Others will rob the garbage pail or drink out of the toilet. Many tiny children have voracious appetites and can put away vast quantities of food, to the amazement of on-lookers. These children are gluttons, wolfing down their meals with arms protectively encircling their plates.

Food Refusal.

While eating voraciously is a most common manifestation of early neglect, refusal to eat is also encountered in some attachment-disordered children. The slow pace of eating (usually severe dawdling — hours spent over each meal), refusal to ask for food or drink, or outright opposition to eating what has been prepared can indicate that the child has attachment problems. The dinner table in this case has likely been a battleground in the past, as we see in the following:

*　*　*　*　*

Morgan sat at the table staring straight ahead, untalking. Though six-years-old, she always seemed to play the same "game" at the table. The foster parents were attempting an experiment. They wanted to see how long Morgan would go without asking for desert. The other children had easily asked for one and then two pieces of pie. Morgan would not ask, although pumpkin pie was her favorite. Her passivity at the table was as predictable as it was baffling to the foster parents. They had repeatedly told her that she could eat what and as much as she wanted.

*　*　*　*　*

Strictly speaking, the case of Morgan does not exemplify food refusal; however, it does hopefully provide an illustration of the stubbornness which often surrounds eating. Refusal to ask for food at the table along with absolute food refusal (in rare cases to the point of starvation) strongly suggests a currently or formerly pathological parent-child relationship, one in which the child's needs were ignored. The power struggle over eating implies that parenting was fraught with insensitivity to the child's needs, tempo, etc. In the most extreme cases, insensitivity evolves into macabre abuse. For example, children have been strapped to their chairs and forced to eat, made to sit staring at their plates for hours. Unbelievably, power struggles of that magnitude might last days or weeks. In a world wherein the child feels completely powerless and insignificant, the dinner table is one area where he can feel powerful, albeit hungry.

Counterfeit Emotionality.

Another symptom of category attachment-disorder, counterfeit emotionality, is manifested in such behaviors as theatrical display; superficial charm; emotional radar; and indiscriminate attachment. As the term implies, the disturbed foster child's emotions are truly counterfeit. He is an emotional imposter, either unaware of how he feels or intent on hiding his feelings from others. When feelings are shown, they are often insincere and manufactured, theatrical and superficial. So too, his relationships are indiscriminate and shallow, as we will see below. The negative working model is again evident in this symptom. With the foster parent, and other adult caretakers, viewed as dangerous, threatening, and rejecting, the maltreated child learns to protect and defend himself physically and psychologically.

Theatrical Display.

Attachment-disordered, foster children have often mastered the art of theatrical display. They can produce emotional responses which are as phoney as a three dollar bill. With Academy Award accuracy, these children fake joy, sadness, love and anger. To these children, fearing intimacy and self-exposure, the expression of true feelings is taboo. Thus, they develop remarkable ability to simulate feeling. Convinced by "good theatre," we are frequently bamboozled, as in the following illustration.

* * * * *

Little Timmy, a wily four-year-old foster child, could cry very convincingly at the preschool. He would feign injury and cry loudly, when in fact, he had struck another child. The preschool staff eventually began to notice that Timmy never cried tears.

* * * * *

The theatrical displays of older, more clever attachment-disordered children are even more deceptive and convincing than those of small kids, like Timmy. Some skilled children can even produce tears at will. Those adults who quickly see through the fakery are in the minority. The foster child, with his winning smile can fake happiness, friendliness or good intentions. The attachment-disordered child can hoodwink the majority of adults, at least at first, with his bogus feelings. However, children and pets may not be so easily deceived.

Commonly, children and family pets detect the fakery first. Children often cut through the deception very quickly because they operate at the level of non-verbal behavior and intuition, while adults can be swept off their feet by an articulate, beguiling child. We adults may provide an easy target because we do not mind it when children are sweet and well-behaved. We are, then, lulled into complacency by the child who, to our face, is pleasant and compliant. By contrast, children and pets may detect the insincerity faster because they are often the first targets for the anger of the foster child. In his fear of adults, the attachment-disordered child may avoid honest expression of emotion towards parent figures, preferring a course of sham, manipulation, and passive resistance. Many foster parents report that, although the child has never verbalized any anger towards them, that he can sometimes be overheard in heated verbal exchanges with other children.

Pets are also quick to discover how bogus these foster children are because they quickly become the hapless targets for suppressed anger. After children and family pets, it is the mother (e.g. foster, adoptive, or group home mother) who next senses something is very wrong with the child.

Superficial Charm.

Aided by superficial charm, the attachment-disordered foster child often easily beguiles non-family members. He makes a good first impression, but one that won't last. Others initially do not recognize how disturbed the child is. They may not see past this child's charisma and apparent candor. They want to believe his stories. Unfortunately, the child can befriend non-family members often for the purpose of avoiding intimate relationships within his foster family, as seen next.

* * * * *

Johnny, a twelve-year-old, foster child, spent a great deal of time across the street with the new neighbors. He charmed them, he joked with them and he poured out his soul, as they sat around the kitchen table. Within the first hour of talking to these neighbors, Johnny had asked this family if he could live with them. He went on to explain, fabricating lies as he went, that his present foster family was abusive and cruel to him. A bruise on his shin was, according to Johnny, the result of a kick by his foster mother. The neighbors, with some misgivings, reported the "abuse" to the local welfare agency.

* * * * *

In these cases, the welfare agency usually finds no abuse, although some attachment-disordered children become targets for abuse in placement. The child's superficial charm along with his ability to tell a convincing lie (see Kleptomania/Compulsive Lying below) creates crises and conflict. It can spoil intimacy and destroy the family's (adoptive or foster) trust in the child. His stories are so credible that various members of the adult world are pitted against each other. The school teacher or psychotherapist, for instance, might be convinced that the foster mother or caseworker acts unreasonably towards the child, who is seen as innocent and mistreated.

Before leaving this subject a word should be said about "mother's intuition." Typically, it is the mother (i.e. foster, adoptive, group home) who has the most powerfully negative feelings (i.e., response and reaction to the child's negative working model and reenactment) towards the child, who professionals only later identify as attachment-disordered. A thorough understanding of the mother's reaction to the child is key to the comprehension of the child's psychopathology. The psychotherapist must listen carefully to the mother's reaction to the child in placement. Subtle, almost invisible communication passes between mother and child, which may escape us as psychotherapists. When mothers suspect that the child's emotions are counterfeit, or when they report feelings of revulsion towards the child, one hypothesis worth considering is that the child makes himself truly repulsive to the mother in some way. We psychotherapists, teachers, caseworkers, friends and neighbors must keep in mind that the child may appear quite different to us. But then, we may have fallen under his spell. We may be victims of counterfeit emotionality.

Thus, when a mother states that affectionate gestures from the child are repugnant to her, the psychologist may discover, upon closer examination, that the child's kisses are, in fact, erotic or that his hugs are mechanical. When a mother feels estranged from a child, we may observe that the child demonstrates emotion in shallow and insincere ways: the laugh is too long, too loud, and too forced; the smile is plastered on and reflexive; crying is theatrical and manipulative. Whatever the behavior, the mother is often aware at some level that the relationship between herself and the child is a sham. We must, therefore, weigh her reactions, careful to avoid viewing the problem as hers. When we are fooled by the child, we might align with him and dismiss the mother's reaction. She may then be perceived by us inaccurately as a cold or rejecting mother.

Emotional Radar.

Children with attachment problems are hyper-alert to what goes on around them interpersonally. They are constantly on the look-out, especially alert around adults. Some of them have an uncanny ability to scan the people around them for trouble, escape routes, and easy marks. Along with this, the attachment-disordered foster child often has an overdeveloped ability to detect what others expect him to say, as we will see in the next case.

* * * * *

Jimmy, a foster child with razor sharp intelligence, could answer questions more evasively than a political candidate. When asked how school was going he would not tell the simple-minded lie that many less disturbed children might. That is, he didn't answer that everything was coming up roses. Jimmy had learned through past contacts with counselors that the therapist wanted to hear about problems. So, he answered, "Not so good." When asked why, Jimmy would proceed to complain about how other children on the playground had been picking on him and getting him into trouble. Jimmy would then turn on the tears in a convincing display of personal agony.

* * * * *

We therapists would usually give our collective right arm to draw out this much feeling from a disturbed child. Pleased with ourselves and truly trying to help, we might be tempted to say reassuringly to a boy like Jimmy, "Now, now...let it out, let it all out." However, what Jimmy had conveniently left out of his tearful litany of complaints was his central role in the abuse he sustained on the playground. He failed to mention that he had provoked one bully by insulting his mother; that he had incited another fight by spreading false rumors about an older student he hated; and that, in general, a wake of trouble followed wherever he passed on the school grounds.

Indiscriminate Attachment.

Attachment-disordered, formerly abused and neglected, foster children show a tendency to indiscriminately relate to others. That is, they fail to discriminate between stranger and friend. As infants, they show no stranger anxiety. As preschoolers, they may walk off with anyone. And as school-aged children, they would go off to live with any adult who might come along. They "attach" prematurely to those whom they barely know, as seen in the following example.

* * * * *

Tara, a bright-eyed, blond-haired, four-year-old foster girl, often astounded and embarrassed the foster mother in public. The child would walk up to total strangers, smile broadly and ask if she could go home with them. The foster mother would sheepishly explain to the strangers that the child belonged to her.

* * * * *

Commonly, children like Tara manifest indiscriminate or premature "attachment" to non-family members. (Attachment may be a misnomer here, since the child's approach of the stranger does not indicate true attachment.) Attachment-disordered children may approach or "attach" to teachers, caseworkers, psychotherapists, and/or neighbors, as Tara singled out strangers. The child who sits on our lap immediately after meeting us, or the child who quickly develops a "special" relationship to psychotherapist, caseworker, or teacher, may be a child with attachment problems.

It is ironic that these foster children often demonstrate the strongest attachment behaviors towards people they hardly know, while they evidence very few signs of attachment in the families to which they are entrusted. It appears that these children prefer relationships with strangers, since those liaisons are much less threatening and demanding. The stranger, in addition, can be put on a pedestal; that is, the child may fantasize that this stranger will provide perfectly for him and his needs.

Often at the beginning of a foster or adoptive placement, the attachment-disordered child will prematurely attach. Foster families often report that the child seemed to blend into the family immediately; that he showed no hesitation in coming to their home; and that he showed no distress in leaving his previous caretakers. The child may have begun to call the foster parents, "Mom and Dad," within moments of arriving in placement. This kind of behavior, as pleasant as it might be to deal with at first, may spell eventual trouble in the placement, once the honeymoon is over. Prematurity of this sort suggests indiscriminate attachment. Over time, this same child may sabotage any true attachment, which is simply too intimate and thus too threatening. Growing close to other human beings is truly a foreign, ominous experience for foster children who are atypically attached.

Kleptomia/Compulsive Lying.

The fourth symptom category of attachment-disorders in children is kleptomania/compulsive lying. Typically, stealing and lying develop together. Deception covers thievery. Trickery conceals robbery. These twin problem behaviors, stealing and lying, effectively dissuade foster parents from trusting the unattached child, who steals and then lies about it, even when caught red-handed. As with other conduct problems, lying and stealing stem fundamentally from a negative working model, i.e. a view of caretakers as unreliable, unresponsive, and too threatening to negotiate needs with.

Chronic Stealing.

Chronic stealing is a cardinal symptom of attachment-disordered children. While essentially normal children may steal during periods of temporary family crises, the disturbed foster child thieves habitually. Viewing the world as stingy, ungiving and unfair, this child feels justified in taking objects as a substitute for affection. Those who work with attachment-disordered foster children soon find out how common stealing is. Indeed, many unsuspecting foster parents, adoptive parents, schoolteachers, therapists, and child care workers have been "ripped off" by foster children.

* * * * *

Barbie, a recently placed foster child, seemed to be a model child in her fourth grade classroom. It seemed a coincidence to her teacher that objects turned up missing throughout the classroom. After three months, however, the teacher discovered where all the missing objects had gone. The bottom of Barbie's desk was layered with extra pencils, notebooks, rulers, and glue which she had squirreled away. No one had ever seen Barbie in the act of stealing.

* * * * *

In the disturbed foster child theft often stems from an underlying, pervasive feeling of deprivation and neglect. This child may experience deep resentment and bitterness over the fact that his needs have been chronically unmet. His resultant negative working model contains no remaining expectation that caretakers might be depended upon to provide for him physically or emotionally, and thus he takes matters into his own hands. As in the case of Barbie, theft of specific objects at home or in school may be a way of expressing hostility towards particular individuals perceived as to blame for gross insensitivity and callousness. Barbie, for instance, was insanely jealous over attention given by the teacher to other children.

In the home, the attachment-disordered child may repeatedly loot the parental bedroom, pilfering jewelry, pocket change, or intimate apparel. It is not uncommon for foster children to steal wedding rings, perhaps in some symbolic way avenging themselves for exclusion from their parents' intimate life. The attachment-disordered child, so desperate for attention, may harbor resentments over the foster parents' private relationship. Each time their bedroom door closes behind them, the child's anger is rekindled.

Kleptomania (that is, compulsive stealing), which may have begun in the family of origin, often generalizes to other settings outside the home, such as school, foster care, the community at large. The child's perception of the world as stingy, exploitive, and unreliable justifies the persistent purloining of anyone's belongings. The habitual act of theft gradually becomes more sophisticated and secretive and gives the child a perverse sense of mastery over others. "Putting one over" on others without getting caught offers the child some temporary satisfaction. Unfortunately, the underlying needs for affection, concern, and appropriate emotional response from loving adults remain unmet. Parent figures become inevitably more distant and more punitive because of the stealing. Stealing exacerbates the problem because it makes it even less likely that the child will ever receive what he needs, i.e. a therapeutic bond to a caring, giving adult. (Thus, we see an unhappy reenactment of the child's early, unfulfilling relationship to his first caretakers recreated in the foster home.)

It should be pointed out that with food stealing as well as with theft of non-nutritional items, the child may have no objective need for whatever is taken. The child's pack-rat behavior, i.e. taking things sometimes randomly without apparent use to him, suggests that it is more the stealing habit and the silent satisfaction of outwitting — and distancing — the stingy adult world that keeps the habit alive.

Pathological Lying.

Pathological lying is the twin sister to chronic stealing. At times lying attempts simply to mislead, as when an untruth serves to hide an act of theft. By lying the child merely seeks to cover his tracks and to either hide or deny that he has stolen something. At other times lying attempts to protect; for example, when the angry, untrusting child deceives others to keep them distant and under his control. The following case illustrates how the child may cover theft with a lie, even when caught redhanded.

* * * * *

J.T. was a convincing liar. His birth father revealed that even when he threatened to beat J.T. with a belt, the boy would not back down from his ridiculous lies. Although at times it was difficult, if not impossible, to disprove J.T.'s excuses, in the most recent episode, the father had caught his son with "the goods." J.T. had not anticipated his father's early return from work, and when he did hear the front door slam, he bolted from the master bedroom, dropping a trail of stolen pocket change, as he ran to his room.

* * * * *

Though caught in the act in this episode, J.T. again would not recant his lies. He tried three slightly different lies on his father to no avail: the other boys stole the money; he was just returning the money which the other boys stole; and (in desperation) the money was his — given to him by an unidentified student at school that day. In addition to the lies told to cover stealing, lies similarly appear when the child has done something wrong, e.g. fought at school, failed to do his homework, etc. When confronted, the child lies simply to hide his wrong-doing.

It is not uncommon for the child to actually believe his own lies and distortions of fact. (It may make it easier for the child to stick to the lie and to elaborate on earlier lies with later ones, if he sincerely comes to believe his own untruths.) Children who lie habitually, even when there is no apparent reason to, may have learned a behavior so thoroughly that they almost cannot unlearn it. Even when given encouragement to "fess up," with promises of immunity from punishment, they steadfastly adhere to their stories.

At other times lying serves more complicated purposes. Lying may occur when there is no specific act to conceal. The child has neither stolen nor done something wrong. In these instances, lying emerges out of a reflexive and nearly unconscious need to conceal — not an act, but the self. In these instances, lying acts to spoil intimacy and trust. That is, lying may serve to keep others at a safe distance from the attachment-disordered foster child who basically distrusts everyone around him. Lying is just one more sign of evasion, withdrawal, and distrust. The child allows nobody in. Lying protects the privacy of his thoughts, feelings, and actions.

Overall, lying provides an excellent way of maintaining psychological distance in relationships with other people. Interestingly, many parents, foster parents, teachers, etc. will tell the deceptive child, "Since you have lied to me in the past, I don't know when I will trust you again." This remark may not be all that punishing for the disturbed foster child who may not want a trust relationship. Interestingly, over time the act of lying itself may become rewarding to the child, who gloats secretly over the gullible adult world which believes him.

(It should be added here that in some cases, the child lies simply out of fear of punishment. Lying became a survival skill in the harshly abusive home, wherein the child was beaten even after admitting the truth. Truth-telling was in no way rewarded, and the child's punishment was not softened to reflect the honesty that followed his crime. One fifth grader told me that after admitting to the theft of two cookies, he was beaten by his father who then himself ate the bag of cookies in front of the boy to teach him a lesson.)

Sexual Obsession and Compulson.

Sexual obsessions and compulsions are common among those children diagnosed as attachment-disordered. Typically, Sexual obsessions/compulsions appear in children who (1) indulge in sexual stimulation in an otherwise understimulating environment; (2) express anger and dominance through sexual acts; and/or (3) are victims of sexual abuse. The list of aberrant sexual behaviors found in troubled foster children includes the following: constant use of vile or sexual language; voyeurism; precocious sexual knowledge; seductive behavior or clothing; excessive public or private masturbation; theft or destruction of other's undergarments; sexual activity with animals; sexual identity disturbances; and molestation and/or attempted or actual sexual intercourse with other children. As seen from the list above, the sexual behavior of foster children may be obsessive, compulsive, perverse, and/or premature.

Sexual behaviors in their foster children are often extremely difficult for foster parents to live with. These behaviors seem linked to a negative working model of the world which views adult caretakers either as exploitive, expecting sexual favors, etc. or as unresponsive and understimulating. We will now discuss several of the more common sexual behaviors. (It should be reiterated here that specific symptoms described herein are not inevitably linked to attachment-disorders. For example, sexual behaviors might derive from exposure to sexual abuse with or without an existing attachment-disorder.)

Seductive Behavior or Clothing.

A child's coy, provocative, and seductive behavior often accompanies the child's attachment disorder. Such behavior also may underscore a history of sexual victimization, as in the following case:

* * * * *

Julie, a winsome, eight-year-old Lolita, immediately alarmed the foster father, when she greeted him the first time they met with a wet "French kiss." Her sexual interest in older males was intense, and she attempted to sit on the lap of her male school teacher, her gym teacher, and any older male visitor to the foster home. After they reported this behavior to the caseworker, he discovered that Julie had indeed been sexually abused by a number of her mother's past boyfriends.

The seductiveness of a child's behavior or dress does not always connote attachment problems, since some children become sexually obsessed without corresponding attachment disorder. However, many disturbed foster children have been sexually victimized, conditioned to act as sexual objects for adults. When they are placed in foster settings or in other living situations, they act in their accustomed ways, to the alarm of the host parent-figures. The negative working model of these children is that caretakers exploit.

Sexual Activity with Other Children.

Foster children frequently victimize or engage other children sexually, well beyond the typical "let's play doctor" encounters. Whereas the normal child might experiment with other children by exhibiting his genitalia, the attachment-disordered child might be expected to go much further. These children might engage in oral-genital contact, sodomy, and sexual intercourse. They might be either leader or "follower" in these sexual encounters. In some cases, foster children invite victimization by older children and in other cases, they victimize younger children. The sexual involvement may be forced or unforced.

* * * * *

Laura, a four-year-old foster child, was found lying on top of the foster parent's three-year-old biological son. Laura would simulate coital movements with this little boy, whenever the foster parents weren't looking.

* * * * *

Sexual activity between the attachment-disordered child and other children may go well beyond Laura's simulated sex acts. Indeed, the foster child can be a serious perpetrator of sexual abuse on other children at home, school, and in the neighborhood. Identifying with those who sexually abused them, these children pass on sexual mistreatment to other victims. Ironically, some attachment-disordered children, rather than actively perpetrating sexual abuse onto others, set themselves up for further abuse by older children and adults. These children seem to attract perpetrators to them and unwittingly foster their own victimization.

Bestiality.

One of the more bizarre forms of sexual obsession/compulsion is bestiality, e.g. sexual activity with animals. Although bestiality is not rare, sexual involvement with animals is quite taboo in this culture. Yet, with surprising frequency foster and adoptive parents report the discovery of sexual behavior between their attachment-disordered child and family pets or farm animals.

The foster parents were obviously shaken and repulsed, as they reported that their eight-year-old foster boy had been encouraging the family dog to "lick his privates." They had been prepared for some sexual acting-out on his part, given his history of victimization. However, they found this macabre act quite unpalatable, and were doubting if they could continue caretaking of this foster child.

Attachment-disordered children have often been subjected to the most harmful and disgusting forms of sexual abuse. Some have been prostituted at a tender age. Others have been victimized by older siblings. Some have been forced into sexual activity with parents, stepparents, siblings, and animals. They have been sexual toys of others and in the process have been introduced to behaviors which later can become fixations.

Passive-Aggression.

The attachment-disordered child is invariably passive-aggressive in some fashion. That is, he exhibits anger in roundabout, underhanded ways. Excessively stubborn, oppositional, and deceitful, he takes control interpersonally while expressing underlying anger in secret, indirect, and/or passive ways, such as: face-to-face compliance with adults along with behind-the-back non-compliance; refusal to answer direct questions; teasing, taunting, and provoking others to rage, while acting innocent or surprised at others' angry reaction; and vengeful acts. The maltreated child learned early-on in life to avoid the direct expression of anger towards parents or other adults. (He views caretakers as threatening, frightening, and rejecting.) Overt, clear expression of anger was ignored, punished, or evoked physical or psychological abuse from parent figures. Accordingly, the child ascertained that vocalization of frustrations, disappointments, and disagreements was fruitless, if not dangerous. Yet, the feelings of anger, frustration, and rage continued within him, suppressed, but building to and seeking for release. Passive-aggression provided a safer avenue for the expression of these pent-up, negative feelings.

Next, we will discuss some of the more common types of passive-aggressive expressions of anger found in attachment-disordered foster children.

Face-to-Face Compliance.

Some foster children give the impression that they intend to do what they are told by adults, but in fact fail to comply. Giving face-to-face compliance, they rebel behind the scenes. Absent is the normal level of argumentation or negotiation seen in adjusted, healthy children. The parent figure or other adult may remain totally unaware of the child's unspoken resistance, until later, as we will see in the following case:

* * * * *

Linda, a constantly smiling, seven-year-old child had been chronically neglected and cruelly abused early in her life. In foster care, she seemed unnaturally agreeable and superficially happy-go-lucky. Linda never argued with her foster parents, nor did she make any demands upon them. And when she was asked to pitch in around the house, she never complained about her assigned chores. However, she also never did her chores. Linda could stand literally for hours with a broom in her hand as she contemplated the dirty floor in the garage.

* * * * *

The typical reaction of the child to doing chores might be one of complaining, whining, or arguing: "But, I didn't mess up the garage — the boys did it; they should clean it up!" In Linda's case, she never vocalized any of the feelings of unfairness. Rather, she simply failed to comply behaviorally. She was a master of "forgetting" to do things around the house, "forgetting" to bring books home from school, and the like. And, if she did attempt to do what she was asked to do, she inevitably "forgot" one or other detail. That is, she would comply only in part. For example, in gym class she would do twenty-four jumping jacks, rather than twenty-five. At home, she would turn the dishwasher on without detergent in it. Thus, even in complying, she was non-compliant — off "by a hair." This pattern became clearer to the foster parents over time and indicated, not a poor memory or lack of understanding, but a pervasive tendency to remain in control and to express non-compliance in silent, subtle ways.

Refusal to Answer Questions.

Many attachment-disordered foster children display abnormalities in verbal communication. They lie, distort, avoid and refuse to answer questions. This abnormal communication may provide a window into the frightening inner world of these highly disturbed children. Many such children refuse to communicate in meaningful ways, preferring to hide behind vague, rambling, or partial answers. They simply refuse to directly answer questions. While not exactly lying (see section on Pathological Lying/Compulsive Stealing above), some children mix half-truths with confusion and babble to come up with a non-answer. Other foster children fall silent altogether, all the while failing to make good eye contact, especially when confronted about their silence.

*   *   *   *   *

Trying to get a simple answer from Toni was an exercise in futility, according to her foster father. He reported, in exasperation, that he grew more confused the more he talked with her. The more confused and frustrated he became, the more Toni's non-answers deteriorated into complete nonsense. Even when he attempted to ask her in completely non-blaming, non-threatening ways about innocuous subjects, Toni appeared to muddy the waters.

*   *   *   *   *

Passive-aggression in communication may serve to express indirectly some anger at the adult world. Many attachment-disordered foster children simply feel safer when the adult world is kept "in the dark." (Note: Some communication problems can be traced to learning disabilities, mental retardation, A.D.H.D., or other neurological disorders. These areas should be evaluated in the foster child.)

Provoking Anger in Others.

Attachment-disordered children often evolve into masterful provocateurs. They expertly tease, taunt, and stimulate others into expressing anger for them. The rage they feel, but do not verbalize, finds expression in the hostility they evoke in others. In the process, other children and adults become the unwitting mouthpiece for this child's unspoken resentments. These others may find themselves frighteningly and unexplainably rage-filled (see Chapter Four), while the attachment-disordered foster child acts the part of the "ultimate innocent" who is mystified by their "overreaction."

*   *   *   *   *

The "first time" foster mother appeared distraught and guilt-ridden, as she confessed to often wanting to beat Tobin, age nine. Unused to such depth of rage, she felt that she was going crazy: "I have never felt like this before around an adult or child. I just have this crazy urge to smack him. He knows just how to get me mad...how to push my buttons. I know I sound like I'm exaggerating; my husband says I've gone off the deep end...It's just a million little things Tobin does or doesn't do that are driving me crazy. It is hard to put it into words exactly. I can't really point to any one thing he has done. And I think he loves it. He gets this "gotcha" grin all over his face, when he's got me furious."

*   *   *   *   *

Although some foster children may provoke anger in glaring, dramatic ways (e.g. by outwardly defiant behavior), others use subtler, unrelenting approaches. They balk at every direction, but never come out in the open with their argument.

They smile constantly and never reveal how they truly feel. They "forget" what they've been told to do. They agree to everything but comply with nothing. Or they appear to comply, but leave out or change some detail. One boy, for example, when told to hang shirts on their hangers, turned them inside out before hanging them.

Wetting and Soiling.

Frequently reported forms of passive-aggression are wetting and soiling, i.e. enuresis and encopresis. In graphic form, disturbed foster children symbolize their anger at the world by, for example, "dumping." These children often have never mastered continence totally, due to the lack of order and guidance from past parent figures. They often engage in battles in the bathroom. They might fail to produce a stool for their parents, but later will defecate in the bedroom. Or they might smear fecal matter on the walls or on themselves. Other children wet their beds or the beds of others; these behaviors are often associated with emotional upset, and specifically with anger.

* * * * *

Every time the foster mother disciplined Larry, age nine, she "paid the piper." Larry, when he felt unfairly censured, silently slipped away to his room, where he would urinate in a corner of the closet. Over time, the foster parents noticed a stench in that room and discovered how angry Larry had been at them.

* * * * *

Attachment-disordered foster children, unable to express anger directly and verbally, often find an outlet in urine and fecal matter. Some children may attempt to hide the evidence of an "accident" by throwing soiled or wet clothing or bedding away. Others appear to want parents to find their dirty underwear hidden in their clean clothes drawer — a smelly, angry "present" to the adult world. (With some children encopresis and enuresis may be less deliberate, more the result of some transient stress or a sign of lack of exposure to toilet training. These symptoms may also have a physical basis, which should be ruled out by a pediatrician or urologist.)

(Note: A common complaint about the child with attachment problems is that he is stubborn, oppositional, resistant, forgetful, headstrong, and unbending to the extreme. Anger in many of these children is expressed in indirect, passive ways which are often excused by comments such as, "I forgot...I didn't know...I didn't hear you...etc." While it is true that many less disturbed children may act and talk the same, it is the quantity, frequency or severity of this passive-aggressive behavior which suggests serious attachment problems.

It should be pointed out that many of the other symptoms mentioned above could be described as forms of passive-aggression. The child who refuses to eat or steals food vengefully, the child who attacks younger children, the child who resists intimacy, and the child who uses sexual behavior to aggravate others, may all be demonstrating passive-aggressive behavior. The symptom of passive aggression is listed separately here because it is often times identified as the chief complaint by parents. Whether the child refuses to make eye contact, deliberately leaves chores incomplete, withholds bowel movements, or urinates down the heat register, it is the passive form of expressing anger which disturbs these parents. Indeed it is the symptom of passive-aggression along with counterfeit emotionality which is at times the least identifiable, yet the most unsettling.

Many parents will almost apologetically report a myriad of minor troubles with the child, which individually appear insignificant but collectively are overwhelming; the child who refuses to respond to a question or answers tangentially, never really addressing the issue; the child who is told to put away the clean dishes and "accidentally" puts them back in the cupboard completely unwashed; the child who soils underwear and hides it in his dresser with the clean stuff. These children may be passive-aggressive. So to are children who withhold the expression of emotion, who remain silent at the table to spite others, and who withdraw from others for days at a time when angry. Whatever the specific behaviors the child uses, the objective is often the same: to avoid direct verbal confrontation with adults or perhaps to evoke anger in the parents. Thus the child with serious attachment problems often contains his own direct expressions of anger, while eliciting it in others.)

Defective Conscience.

The last symptom of attachment-disorder is that of defective conscience, which includes the lack of guilt or remorse and denial of — or projection of — blame.

Absence of Guilt.

The attachment-disordered, child often feels little guilt or regret. When caught shoplifting, for example, he feels remorseless. If upset at all, it is because he has been caught and punished, not because he has broken a rule or disappointed his parents. The normal sense of personal guilt and responsibility is lacking, as seen in the following case:

* * * * *

The foster parents of Mark were most upset about what they called his "cold-heartedness." An abused and neglected, six-year-old boy, he frequently abused a younger foster boy in the home. He deliberately pushed him down an escalator, pulled out large clumps of his hair in fights, and once struck this younger boy in the head with a lead pipe. When caught and punished, Mark cried (without tears) but seemed to feel no remorse. Although the adoptive parents directed him to apologize to this younger child, Mark refused.

* * * * *

Foster (and adoptive) parents commonly report that their children demonstrate an eerie lack of remorse. These children appear strangely indifferent to the most heinous acts. While these parents can train the child to apologize for misbehavior, they often do not see any improvement in moral development.

Denial and Projection of Blame.

Hand in hand with the absence of guilt, goes the disturbed foster child's use of denial and projection of blame. Denial and projection are twin psychological defenses used most commonly by the attachment-disordered child. Armed with these defenses, the child staunchly wards off feelings of personal responsibility and directs blame onto others, as in the following case example:

* * * * *

Johnny admitted that he had been playing with matches and some kindling, but he denied that it was his fault that the shed burned down. He said that nothing would have happened, if the wind had not been blowing. Then he added that it was the foster mother's fault for calling him for supper, just when he was going to stomp out the smoldering ashes. He obviously believed he was blameless. Indeed, he seemed truly angry at the foster mother for her part in the fire.

* * * * *

Denial and projection of blame, as seen in the case of Johnny, differ from simple lying (see Lying and Stealing above). For example, Johnny admitted to the facts of the case. However, he automatically and perhaps unconsciously resorted to the use of the twin defenses. Reflexively he acted to absolve himself of any feelings of guilt or remorse. It was obvious to him that his foster mother's call to dinner caused the shed to burn down. Clearly, Johnny felt blameless in the matter, as his conscience lay sleeping. We include this discussion of denial and projection here because they are the defenses which appear in place of expected feelings of guilt. Johnny and other attachment-disordered children develop these defenses to the detriment of normal conscience formation.

Index